Internet of Things (IoT)

The Authors

Dr. S. Anandamurugan obtained his Bachelor's degree in Electrical and Electronics Engineering from "Maharaja Engineering College, Avinashi" under Bharathiyar University and Masters Degree in Computer Science and Engineering from "Arulmigu Kalasalingam College of Engineering, Krishnan Koil" under Madurai Kamaraj University. He completed his Ph.D in Wireless Sensor Networks under Anna University, Chennai. He has 17 years of teaching experience. He is currently working as an Assistant Professor (Selection Grade) in the Information Technology department of Kongu Engineering College. He got 10 awards. Received "Dr.A.P.J.Abdul Kalam award for Teaching Excellence" award for the year 2017 - 2018 from Marina Labs, Chennai. Received "Best Outstanding faculty" award for the year 2016 - 2017 from Top Engineers, Chennai. Received "Teaching Excellence" award for the year 2016 - 2017 from Indus Foundation, Chennai. Received "Senior Educator and Researcher" award for the year 2016 - 2017 from National Foundation for Entrepreneurship Development, Coimbatore. Received "Outstanding Faculty" award for the year 2016 - 2017 from Venus International Foundation, Chennai. Received "UWA Effluent Star of the Decade" award for the year 2016 - 2017 from CHAPTERed Writers Association, Chennai. Received "Best Paper" award for the year 2016 from International Journal for Modern Trends in Science and Technology (ISSN:2455-3778) for the paper entitled on "An Energy-Efficient Min-Max Optimization with RSA Security in Wireless Sensor Networks". Received "Best Author" award for the year 2012 - 2013 from Shivam Book Publishers, Chennai. Received "Best Staff" award for the year 2007 - 2008 at Kongu Engineering College, Perundurai. Received "Appreciation award" for producing excellent result in Anna University examinations held in Nov/Dec 2003 by Kongu Engineering College (Citation plus reward). Project entitled on "Automated Irrigation System using Wireless Sensor Networks" selected as a best project by Kongu Engineering College in 2015-2016. Industrial Training attended: 3. Seminar/Workshop Conducted: 10. Conference Organized: 5. Value Added Course conducted: 5. Sponsored Projects carried out: 1, Consultancy Activities: 6. He has written 75 books under various titles and publications. Three of his books are prescribed as Text/Reference books by many leading Universities and autonomous Colleges in India. The book titled on "Wireless Sensor Networks" published by University Science Press, New Delhi is referred in the syllabus of JNTUK and its affiliated colleges, GMR Institute of Technology, Kakinada. The book titled on "Wireless Sensor Networks" published by Satya Prakashan Publisher, New Delhi is referred in the syllabus of University of Mysore. The book titled on "Placement Interviews: Skills For Success" , McGraw Hill, New Delhi is referred in the syllabus of JNTUH and its affiliated colleges, All Branches of KIIT University, Bhubaneswar, Odisha, Dr.M.G.R. Educational and Research Institute University, Chennai, Madanapalle Institute of Technology & Science, Madanapalle, AP (Autonomous), Mari Laxman Reddy Group of Institutions, Teungana, Charustar University of Science and Technology, Gujarat, Bharathiyar University, Coimbatore and Paavai Engineering College, Namakkal, Tamilnadu.

P. S.Nandhini obtained her Bachelor's degree in Information Technology from "Avinashilingam Institute for Home Science and Higher Education for Women-Coimbatore" under Avinashilingam University and Masters Degree in Computer and Communication Engineering from "Kongu Engineering College – Perundurai" under Anna University. Currently she is doing PhD under Anna University and working as an Assistant Professor in the department of Computer Science Engineering in Kongu Engineering College, Perundurai. She is a life member of CSI. Her area of interest includes Wireless Networks and Network Security. She has attended Seminars and Workshops organized by various Engineering colleges. She has published papers in International and National Journals and also in International and National Conferences.

Internet of Things (IoT)

Dr. S. Anandamurugan

Ms. P. S. Nandhini

School of Communication and Computer Sciences
Kongu Engineering College
Perundurai, Erode, Tamilnadu, India

2019

Associated Publishing Company®

A Division of

Astral International Pvt. Ltd.

New Delhi – 110 002

ISBN: 9789390384259 (HB)

Publisher's Note:

Every possible effort has been made to ensure that the information contained in this book is accurate at the time of going to press, and the publisher and author cannot accept responsibility for any errors or omissions, however caused. No responsibility for loss or damage occasioned to any person acting, or refraining from action, as a result of the material in this publication can be accepted by the editor, the publisher or the author. The Publisher is not associated with any product or vendor mentioned in the book. The contents of this work are intended to further general scientific research, understanding and discussion only. Readers should consult with a specialist where appropriate.

Every effort has been made to trace the owners of copyright material used in this book, if any. The author and the publisher will be grateful for any omission brought to their notice for acknowledgement in the future editions of the book.

Published by : **Associated Publishing Company®**
A Division of
Astral International Pvt. Ltd.
– ISO 9001:2015 Certified Company –
4736/23, Ansari Road, Darya Ganj
New Delhi-110 002
Ph. 011-43549197, 23278134
E-mail: info@astralint.com
Website: www.astralint.com

Preface

IoT (Internet of Things) is an advanced automation and analytics system which exploits networking, sensing, big data, and artificial intelligence technology to deliver complete systems for a product or service. These systems allow greater transparency, control, and performance when applied to any industry or system.

IoT systems have applications across industries through their unique flexibility and ability to be suitable in any environment. They enhance data collection, automation, operations, and much more through smart devices and powerful enabling technology. This book aims to provide you with a thorough introduction to IoT. It introduces the key concepts of IoT, necessary in using and deploying IoT systems.

Authors

Contents

1

Introduction to IoT

Introduction

Now-a-days, around two to three billions of people around the world use the Internet for browsing the web, using social networking applications, posting and receiving emails, accessing multimedia content and services, playing games and many other tasks. Many people gain access to global information and communication infrastructure and another big leap is coming forward related to the use of Internet as a global platform for enabling machines and smart objects communicate, dialogue, compute and coordinate. It is suspected that within the next decade the Internet will exist as a seamless fabric of classic networks and networked objects. The service and the content will be around us, always available, paving the way to new applications, enabling new ways of working, interacting, entertainment and the way of living. In such a perspective, the concept of the Internet as an infrastructure network reaching out to end-users' terminal will vanish, leaving space to notion of interconnected "Smart" objects forming pervasive computing environments. The infrastructure of the Internet will retain its vital role as global backbone for worldwide information sharing and diffusion, interconnecting physical object with computing or communication capabilities across a wide range of services and technologies.

This innovation will be executed by embedding electronics into everyday physical object, making them "smart" and integrating them within global infrastructure. This will give rise to new opportunities for the Information and Communication Technologies sector, paving the way to new services and applications thus leveraging the interconnection of physical and virtual realms. Many think of the IoT as a single global network. But the IoT actually encompasses a multiple independent and complementary networks in various service sectors such as efficient energy distribution and usage, home automation systems, vehicular traffic management and healthcare services.

- ★ The Internet of Things (IoT) is used to refer

- The resulting global network interconnecting smart objects by means of extended Internet Technologies
- The set of supporting technologies (RFIDs, sensor/actuators, machine-to-machine communication devices, *etc.*,) to realise the vision
- The ensemble of applications and services leveraging the above technologies to open up business and market opportunities

It is an information network connecting virtual and physical objects. The main strength of the IoT idea is the high impact that it will have on several aspects of everyday-life and behaviour of potential users. The effects of the IoT introduction will be visible in both industry and domestic fields.

Definition

The Internet of Things (also referred to as ***Internet of Everything or IoE***) refers to the multiple networks of devices (things) or technology platform that communicate with each other via wireless protocols without human intervention. The connections made through IoT enabled device facilitate the rapid and efficient transfer of data needed to support a wide range of activities and operations. In this way, the application of IoT technologies can lead to significant operational improvements such as increased efficiency, better performance and enhanced safety

Three Cs of IoT

The three Cs of IoT are

- Communication
- Control and Automation
- Cost Saving

Communication

IoT communicates information such as state and data from sensor to people and systems. For example GPS-enabled assets can communicate their current location and movement. Location is important for the items that move such as trucks but it is also applicable for locating items and people within an organisation. In the healthcare industry, IoT can help a hospital track the location of everything from wheelchairs to surgeons. In the transport industry, a business can deliver real-time tracking and condition of parcels and pallets.

Control and Automation

In the connected world, the business will have the visibility into the device's condition. In many cases, consumer or device itself will be able to control a device remotely. For example, a business can remotely turn on or shut down a specific piece of equipment or adjust the temperature in a climate-controlled environment. The user can also use IoT to unlock their car or start the refrigerator. If the performance baseline has been established, a process can send alerts or notification for anomalies and possibly deliver an automated response.

For example: The farmer gets alert or notification if the water in the well is about to be emptied.

Cost Savings

Most of the companies adopt IoT to earn and save money. The measurements provided by the devices are actual performance of the data instead of just estimates. There is also a disadvantage that industrial companies lose money when equipments fail. With new sensor information, IoT can help a company to save money by minimising the failure of the equipment and allowing the business to perform the planned maintenance. Sensor can also measure iyems such as driving behaviour and speed, reduce fuel expenses, wear and tear on consumables. The smart meters in home and businesses can provide data that help people understand the consumption of energy and opportunities for cost savings.

2. Characteristics of IoT

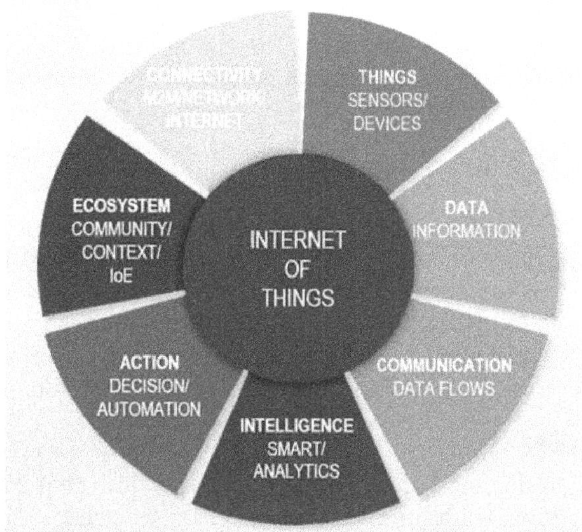

CHARACTERISTICS OF IoT

1. Connectivity

Connectivity supports IoT by bringing together everyday objects or things. Connectivity of these objects is important because simple object level interactions contribute towards overall intelligence in IoT network. It enables network accessibility and compatibility in the things. With this connectivity, new market opportunities for IoT can be created by the networking of smart things/devices and applications. IoT devices can have *self-configuring capability* which allow large of devices to work together to provide certain functionality. IoT devices may support a number of *interoperable communication protocols* and can communicate with other devices and also infrastructure.

2. Intelligence

IoT is smart with the combination of

- ✯ Algorithms
- ✯ Software
- ✯ Hardware and
- ✯ Computational capabilities

Ambient intelligence in IoT enhances its capabilities which facilitate the things to respond in an intelligent way to a particular situation and supports the device in carrying out specific tasks. In spite of all the popularity of smart technologies, intelligence in IoT is only concerned as means of interaction between devices, while user and device interaction is achieved by standard input methods and graphical user interface

3. Dynamic Nature

IoT devices and systems may have the changing capability to dynamically adapt with the changing contexts and take actions based on their

- ✯ Operating conditions
- ✯ User's context or
- ✯ Sensed environment

The primary activity of Internet of Things is to sense the data and collect it from its environment. This is achieved with the dynamic changes that take place around the devices. The state of the devices changes dynamically. Example: Sleep and Awake, Connected and/or Disconnected, *etc*. In addition to the state of the device, the number of devices also changes dynamically with a person, place and time

4. Enormous Scale

The number of devices that need to be managed and that communicate with each other will be much larger than the devices connected to the cInternet. The management of data generated from these devices and their interpretation for application purposes becomes more critical. Gartner (2015) confirms the enormous scale of IoT in the estimated report where it stated that 5.5 million new things will get connected every day and 6.4 billion connected things will be in use worldwide in 2016, which is up by 30 percent from 2015. The report also forecasts that the number of connected devices will reach 20.8 billion by 2020.

5. Sensing

IoT wouldn't be possible without sensors. It is used to detect or measure any changes in the environment to generate data that can report on their status or even interact with the environment. Sensing technologies provide the means to create capabilities that reflect a true awareness of the physical world and the people in it. The sensing information is simply the analog input from the physical world, but it can provide the rich understanding of the complex world.

6. Heterogeneity

Heterogeneity in Internet of Things is one of the key characteristics. Devices in IoT are based on different hardware platforms and networks and can interact with other devices or service platforms through different networks. IoT architecture should support direct network connectivity between heterogeneous networks. The key design requirements for heterogeneous things and their environments in IoT are

- Scalabilities
- Modularity
- Extensibility and
- Interoperability

7. Security

IoT devices are naturally vulnerable to security threats. There is a high level of transparency and privacy issues with IoT. It is important to secure the endpoints, the networks, and the data that is transferred across all of it means creating a security paradigm

8. Unique Identity

Each IoT device has a unique identity as well as unique identifier such as IP address. IoT system may have intelligent interfaces which adapt based on the context, allow communicating with users and the environmental context. IoT device interfaces allow communicating with users and environmental contexts. IoT interfaces allow

- Users to query the device
- Monitor their status
- Controlling them remotely

9. Integration into Information Network

IoT devices are usually integrated into the information network that allows them to communicate and exchange data with other devices and systems. IoT devices can be dynamically discovered in the network by other devices or the network. It also have the capability to describe themselves to other devices or user applications. Integration into the information network helps in making IoT systems "smarter" due to collective intelligence of the individual devices in collaboration with the infrastructure.

There are a wide variety of technologies that are associated with Internet of Things that facilitate in its successful functioning. IoT technologies possess the above-mentioned characteristics which create value and support human activities; they further enhance the capabilities of the IoT network by mutual cooperation and becoming the part of the total system.

3. Physical Design of IoT

1. Things in IoT

IoT devices in the Internet of Things are nonstandard computing devices that connect wirelessly to a network and have the ability to transmit data. The things have unique identity and can perform remote sensing, actuation and monitoring capabilities. IoT devices can exchange data with other connected devices. It can process the data either locally or send the data to centralised servers or cloud based application for processing the data.

The Things may provide:

- ★ Identification and information storage (RFID tags, MAC address)
- ★ Information collection (Sensor networks, store sensor values)
- ★ Information processing (Understanding commands, filtering data)
- ★ Communications (Transmit and receive messages)
- ★ Actuation (Switch control, motor control)

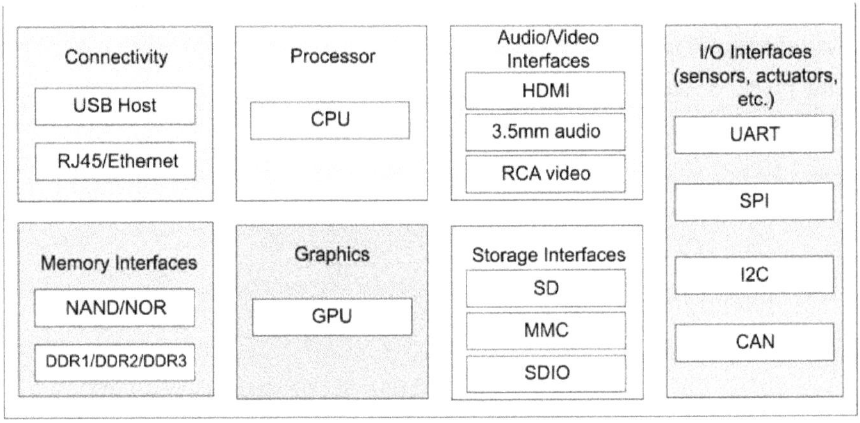

Block Diagram of IoT Device

An IoT device consists of onbord sensors or attached sensors. It collects various types of data from the sensors. The sensed data can be communicated to other devices or cloud for storage. There are several interfaces for connection of wired and wireless devices. These include

- ★ I/O interfaces for sensor
- ★ Interface for Internet connectivity
- ★ Memory and storage interfaces
- ★ Audio/video interfaces

IoT devices can be of wearable sensors, smart watches, LED lights, automobiles and industrial machines.

2. IoT protocols

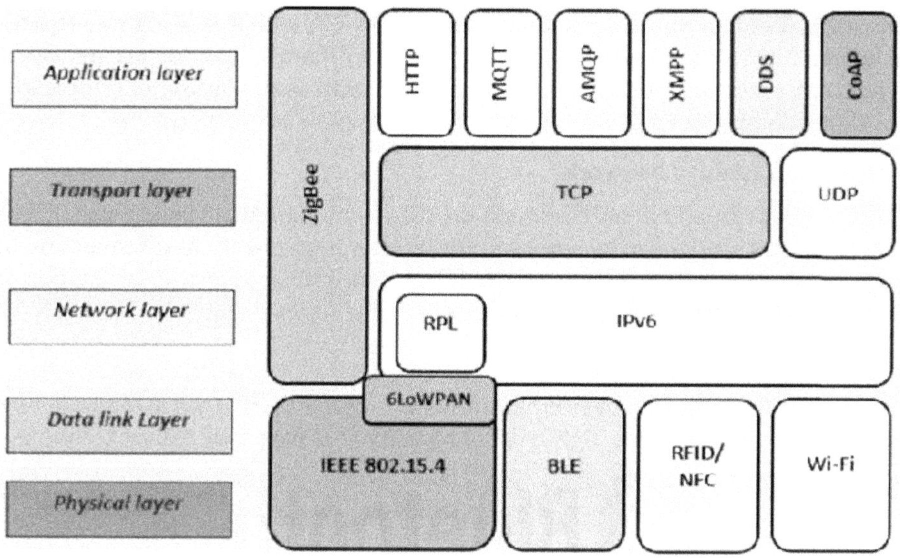

IoT Data Link Protocol

It deals with physical and logical layer protocols that are used for connection establishment.

1. IEEE 802.15.4

IEEE 802.15.4 is the most commonly used IoT standard for MAC. It defines how nodes can communicate with each other. It is used for forming Personal Area Network which is a low data rate network. The data rate has to be monitored and controlled for extending the life time of the network. The frame formats used in traditional networks are not suitable for low power multi-hop networking in IoT due to their overhead. It uses time synchronization and channel hopping to enable high reliability, low cost and meet IoT communications requirements. It uses DSSS (Direct Sequence Spread Spectrum) modulation. It uses CSMA/CA (Carrier sense multiple Access/Collision avoidance) mechanism for channel access. It supports multiplexing (Multiple nodes interference free access to same channel at different times). The transmission range is 10m to75m. The best transmission range achieved in outdoor

IEEE 802.15.4 features:

- ✯ Highly tolerant to noise and interference
- ✯ Link reliability mechanism

IEEE 802.15.4 Types:

- ✯ Beacon Enabled Network
- ✯ Non-Beacon Enabled Network

Beacon Enabled Network

In Beacon enabled network, there is a periodic transmission of beacon message. The data frames sent via slotted CSMA/CA with a super frame structure managed by PAN (Personal Area Network) Coordinator. The beacons are used for synchronisation and association of other nodes with the Coordinator. The scope of operation spans the whole network

Non-Beacon Enabled Network

In Non-Beacon Enabled Network, the data frames are sent via unslotted CSMA/CA. In this network beacons are used for link layer discovery to discover any link from one device to another and so on. It requires both source and destination Ids. It provides decentralised communication among nodes

2. BLE (Bluetooth Low Energy)

Bluetooth is a short range communication protocol used to transfer data between mobile devices. It ensures high level of security. It is based on Adhoc technology.

Bluetooth™

An important term in the context of Bluetooth is a **piconet.** A piconet is a collection of Bluetooth devices which are synchronised to the same *hopping sequence.* One device in the piconet can act as *Master (M)* and all the other devices as *Slave (S).* The Master determines the hopping pattern in the piconet and the slaves have to synchronise to this pattern. Each piconet has a unique hopping pattern. *Parked device* can't actively participate in the piconet but are known and can be reactivated within some milliseconds. More than 200 devices can be parked. Only 8 devices can be active ($2^3 = 8$) *i.e.,* 3-bit address are used in Bluetooth. Forming group of piconets is called **Scatternets.**

3. RFID: *Radio Frequency Identification*

In RFID tags data are digitally encoded in RFID tags and can be read by a reader. It is similar to barcode and QR codes but functionality or operation is different. The tags can be *active or passive.* Active tags own a little power supply. It works on the principle of induction. Inductively when passive tags come in proximity to the RFID reader, the magnetic force fields are created due to which information is transferred between two devices.

Working Principles

It is derived from Automatic Identification and Data Capture technology (AIDC) which is a wired technology. AIDC performs

- ⋆ Object Identification
- ⋆ Object data collection
- ⋆ Mapping of collected data to computer with little or human intervention

RFID uses radio waves to perform ADC functions. RFID includes the following components

- ★ RFID tag/Smart label
- ★ RFID Reader
- ★ Antenna

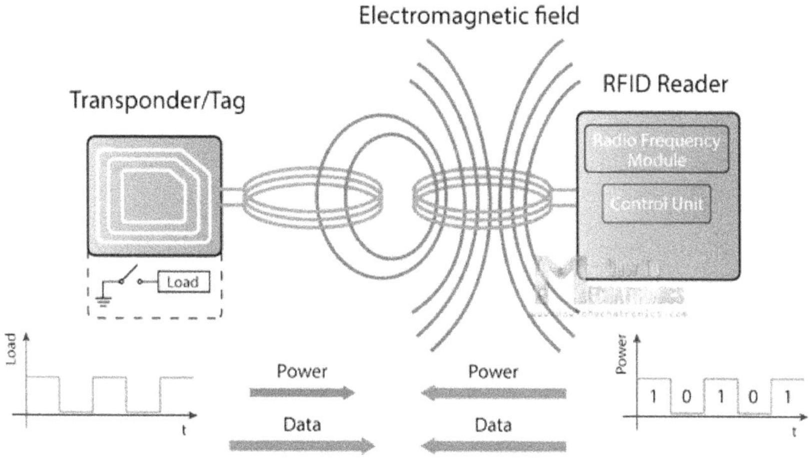

The antenna emits radio signals to activate the tag and to read and write data to it. Depending upon its power output and the radio frequency used, the reader emits radio waves in ranges of one inch to 100 feet or more. When an RFID tag passes through the electromagnetic zone, it detects the reader's activation signal. The reader decodes the data encoded in the tag's integrated circuit (silicon chip) and the data is passed to the host computer for processing. The purpose of an RFID system is to enable data to be transmitted by a portable device, called a *tag,* which is read by an RFID reader and processed according to the needs of a particular application. The data transmitted by the tag may provide identification or location information or specifics about the product tagged, such as price, colour, date of purchase, *etc.* RFID quickly gained attention because of its ability to track moving objects. A typical RFID tag consists of a microchip attached to a radio antenna mounted on a substrate. The chip can store as much as 2 kilobytes of data. To retrieve the data stored on an RFID tag, reader is needed. A typical reader is a device that has one or more antennas that emit radio waves and receive signals back from the tag. The reader then passes the information in digital form to a computer system. Once a link is established with a unique ID on an item, then automation of an assortment of processes ensures.

Applications

- ★ Asset tracking
- ★ Personal tracking (Attendance)
- ★ ID badging

- ★ Supply chain management
- ★ Controlling Access to restricted areas
- ★ Counterfeit prevention(in the pharmaceuticals)

4. Near Field Communication (NFC)

NFC is similar to RFID. It is based on *magnetic induction* between card and the reader. It is designed for use by device within close proximity to each other. The communication range is less than 20cm.It is used to communicate data such as Identification Number, Status information and any other information. It has three modes of operation

- ★ Peer to Peer
- ★ Read/write
- ★ Card emulation

Applications

- ★ Smart phone based payments
- ★ Parcel tracking
- ★ Information tag in posters and ad
- ★ Toys
- ★ Low power home automation

Network Layer

1. RPL (Routing Protocol for Low Power and Lossy Network)

RPL is based on Distance Vector Routing. It maintains the routing topology using low rate beaconing. The beaconing rate increases on detecting inconsistencies *i.e.,* node or link failure in the network. The routing information is included in datagram itself. RPL separates the packet forwarding and processing information from routing optimisation objective. The routing optimisation objectives are

- ★ Minimising energy
- ★ Reducing latency
- ★ Satisfying constraints with respect to node power, bandwidth, *etc.,*

RPL supports confidentiality and integrity. It supports data validation and loop detection. It operates using bidirectional links but in lossy scenario the links may exhibit *asymmetric* property. Asymmetric means the source sends the packet in one route may be directly but due to environmental condition, the response may take other direction. The reachability of a router is verified before the router can be used as a parent. The routing can be of two types:

- ★ Proactive: Maintains routing topology
- ★ Reactive: Resolving routing inconsistencies

2. IPv6: Internet Protocol version 6

IPv6 is the newest version of Internet protocol and successor to IPv4. IPV6 uses 128-bit address that allows total of 2^{128} address. The initial design of IPv4 did not anticipate the following conditions:

- Recent exponential growth of the Internet and the impending exhaustion of the IPv4 address space
- The ability of Internet backbone routers to maintain large routing tables
- Need for simpler auto-configuration and re-numbering
- Requirement for security at the IP level (IPSec)
- Need for better support for real-time delivery of data, known as quality of service (QoS)

Advantages of IPv6

The following are the advantages of IPv6:

- Simplified header format for efficient packet handling
- Larger payload for increased throughput and transport efficiency
- Hierarchical network architecture for routing efficiency
- Support for widely deployed routing protocols (OSPF, BGP, *etc.*)
- Auto-configuration and plug-and-play support
- Elimination of need for network address translation (NAT) and application layered gateway (ALG)
- Increased number of multicast addresses

Transport Layer Protocol

1. TCP

Transmission Control Protocol is a transport layer protocol that is used by web browsers, email programs and file transfer. TCP is a connection oriented and stateful protocol. TCP ensures reliable transmission of packets in-order. TCP also provides *error detection* capability so that duplicate packets can be discarded and lost packets are retransmitted. The flow control capability of TCP ensures that are at a rate at which the sender sends the data is not too high for the receiver process. The congestion control capability of TCP avoids network congestion.

2. UDP

UDP is a connectionless protocol. It is useful for time-sensitive application that have very small data units to exchange and don't want the overhead of connection setup. UDP is a *transaction oriented and stateless protocol.* UDP doesn't guarantee delivery, ordering of messages and duplicate elimination. Higher level of protocols can ensure reliable delivery or ensuring connections created reliable.

Application Layer Protocol

1. HTTP

HTTP (Hyper Text Transfer Protocol) is the application layer protocol that forms the foundation of the WWW (World Wide Web). Its port number is 80. A web HTTP server listens to port 80 and responds to 80 only. An HTTPS (HTTP over Secure Socket Layer or TLS) port number is 443. HTTP is a *stateless protocol* and each request is independent of other requests. It means there is no session or sequence number field or no field that is retained in the next exchange.

Features

1. The HTTP protocol is light weight protocol and thus speedy as compared to other protocols. HTTP is able to transfer any type of data to a client provided it is capable of handling that data
2. The HTTP protocol is flexible. If any connection breaks occur during communication, the client can start by re-connecting. Being a stateless protocol, HTTP does not keep track of the state
3. A provision of user authentication exists besides the basic authentication
4. HTTP protocol is based on Object Oriented Programming System (OOPS). Methods are applied to objects identified by a URL
5. Status codes add in response and caching of a resource provided at a server.
    - ★ 400- Bad Request
    - ★ 401-Unauthorised Request
    - ★ 402-Request requires a payment before response is feasible
    - ★ 403-Request is for a forbidden resource
    - ★ 404-URL resource not found by the server

The HTTP specific methods are

- ★ GET
- ★ POST
- ★ HEAD
- ★ CONNECT
- ★ PUT
- ★ DELETE
- ★ TRACE
- ★ OPTIONS

2. MQTT: Message Queue Telemetry Transport

Telemetry- Sending message to far off place by radio or other mechanism

It is a light-weight message protocol based on *Publish-Subscribe* model. It can be used in conjunction with TCP/IP protocol. It offers connectivity (mostly embedded) between applications and middleware on one side and network communication on the other side. MQTT uses a *client-server architecture* where the client connects to the server and publishes the messages to the topics on the server. *A message broker* controls the publish-subscribe messaging pattern. A *topic* to which a client is subscribed is updated in the form of message and distributed by message broker. It is suited for constrained environment where the devices have limited processing power and resources

Designed for

- Remote Connection
- Limited Bandwidth
- Small code footprint

MQTT components

1. Publishers
2. Subscribers
3. Brokers

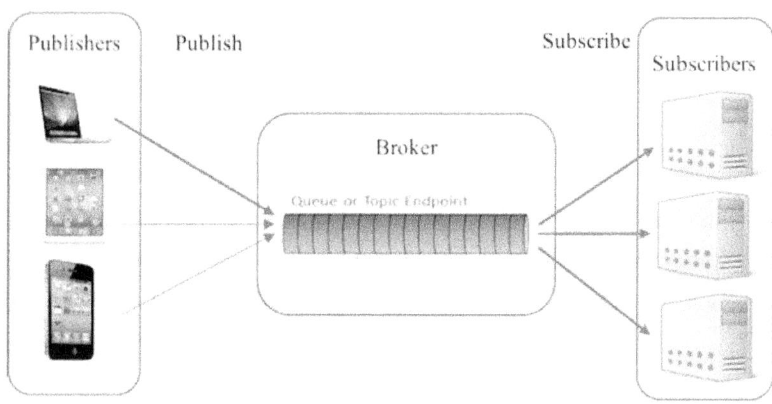

MQTT Broker does the following:

1. Functions as a server, capable of storing messages from publishers and forwarding them to the subscribed clients
2. Stores the topics received from the publisher and forwards them to subscribers
3. Receives subscriptions from clients on the topics, matches subscriptions and publications in order to route message to right nodes.
4. Recovers subscriptions on reconnect after a disconnection, unless the client is explicitly disconnected
5. Acts as a broker between the publisher of the topics and their subscribers

6. Finds client disconnection until DISCONNECT message is received, keeps message alive till explicit disconnection
7. Retains the last-received message from a publisher for a new connected subscriber on the same topic, when retain field in the header is set
8. Authentication by Username/Password in connect message and client security is through SSL/TLS. Security considerations are same as of CoAP, web-linking and CoRE resource directory
9. Support from Intelligent and business analyst server and other servers through a MQTT server with a gateway

MQTT methods

1. Connect
2. Disconnect
3. Subscribe
4. Unsubscribe
5. Publish

Applications of MQTT

1. Facebook Messenger for online chat
2. Amazon web services uses Amazon IoT with MQTT
3. Microsoft Azure IoT hub uses MQTT as its main protocol for telemetry message
4. The everything IoT platform uses MQTT as an M2M protocol for millions of connected products
5. Adafruit launched a free MQTT cloud service for IoT experiments called AdafruitIO

SMQTT

An extension of MQTT is Secure MQTT (SMQTT). SMQTT is proposed only to enhance the security features of MQTT. It uses *encryption* based on *lightweight attribute based encryption*. The main advantage of using this encryption is the broadcast encryption feature, in which one message is encrypted and delivered to multiple other nodes and this is quite common in IoT applications.

In general, the algorithm consists of four main stages:

- Setup: The publishers register themselves to the broker and get a master secret key according to their developer's choice of key generation algorithm
- Encryption: The published data is encrypted. The key generation and encryption algorithms are not standardized.
- Publish: Published by the broker which sends it to the subscribers

- Decryption: Finally decrypted at the subscribers which have the same master secret key.

3. AMQP: Advanced Message Queuing Protocol

AMQP defines how business messages are passed between Applications/ Organisations. It connects between systems and business processes. AMQP supports functional interoperability between conforming clients and messaging middleware servers (also called "brokers"). It is based on ISO/IEC 19464. The basic unit of data is frame (not linked with frame in link layer, it is different). It is designed for financial industry. It runs over TCP and provides a publish/subscribe architecture which is similar to that of MQTT. The difference is that broker is divided into two main components:

- Exchange : Responsible for receiving publisher message and distributing them to queues based on pre-defined roles and conditions
- Queue : Represent the topics and subscribed by subscribers which will get the sensory data whenever they are available in the queue

Scope of AMQP

To enable interoperability for messaging middleware requires both the networking protocol and the semantics of the server-side services. AMQP, therefore, defines both the network protocol and the server-side services through:

- A defined set of messaging capabilities called the "*Advanced Message Queuing Protocol Model*" (AMQ model). The AMQ model consists of a set of components that route and store messages within the broker service, plus a set of rules for wiring these components together
- *A network wire-level protocol*, AMQP, that allows the client applications talk to the server and interact with the AMQ model it implements

AMQP ensures

- Reliability of message deliveries
- Rapid and ensured delivery of messages
- Message acknowledgements

AMQP components

The components of AMQP are:

- **Exchange:** A part of the broker (*i.e.* server) which receives messages and routes them to queues
- **Queue (message queue):** A named entity which messages are associated with and from where consumers receive them
- Bindings: Rules for distributing messages from exchanges to queues

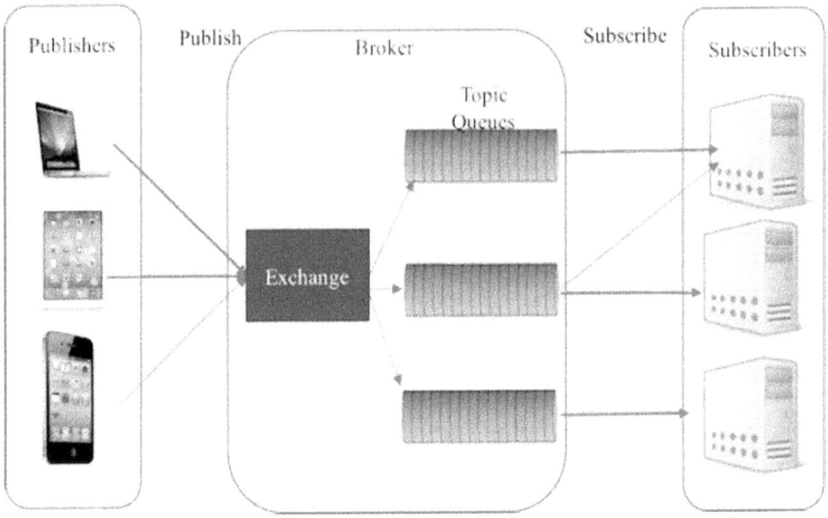

AMQP Frame Types

There are nine frame types that are used to begin, control and tear down the transfer of message between two peers. The frame types are

- ★ Open: To open connection
- ★ Begin: To begin the session
- ★ Attach: To initiate new link
- ★ Transfer: To send actual message
- ★ Flow: To control message flow rate
- ★ Disposition: To inform the change in state of transfer
- ★ Detach: To terminate the link
- ★ End: To close the session
- ★ Close: To close the connection

Applications

- ★ Monitoring and global update sharing
- ★ Connecting different system and processes to talk to each other
- ★ Allowing server to respond to immediate requests quickly and delegate time consuming tasks for later processing
- ★ Distributing a message to multiple recipients for consumption
- ★ Enabling offline clients to fetch data at a later time
- ★ Introducing fully asynchronous functionality for systems
- ★ Increasing reliability and uptime of application deployment

4. XMPP: Extensible Messaging and Presence Protocol

XMPP is an open standard communication protocol for message oriented middleware based on XML. It is used for real time exchange of structured data. It uses ***client-server architecture***. It provides the facilities for discovery of services residing locally or across the network and the availability information of these services. It is well suited for cloud computing (due to discovery of service).

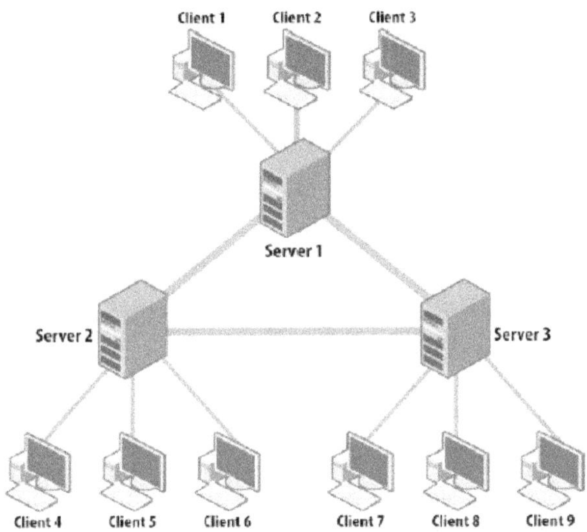

Client-Server Architecture

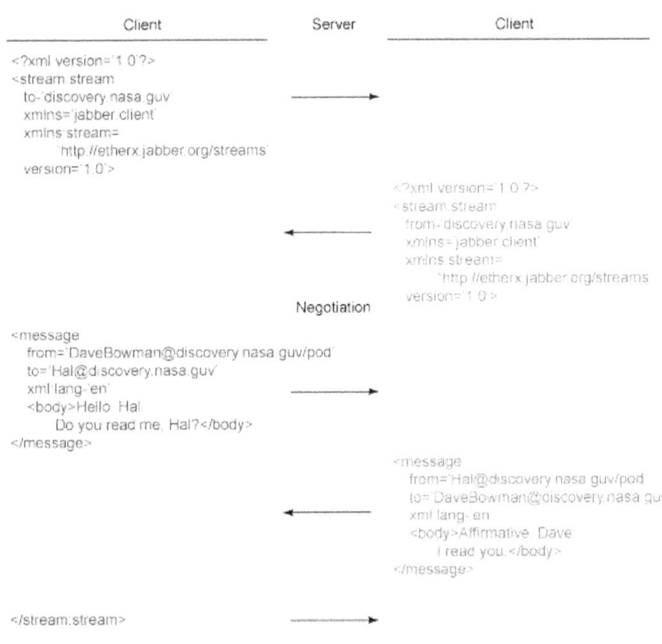

Simplified XMPP Communication

Technologies of XMPP

- Core: It is used to provide information about core XMPP technologies for XML streaming
- Jingle: Multimedia signalling for voice and video file transfer
- Multi-user chat: Flexible, multi-party communication
- PubSub: Alerts or notification for data syndication
- BOSH: It is used to provide HTTP binding for XMPP

Advantages of XMPP

- No central server *i.e.,* anyone can run their own XMPP server(***Decentralisation***)
- It is an ***open standard*** *i.e.,* No royalties or permission are required to implement the specifications
- It provides ***security mechanism*** such as authentication, encryption, *etc*
- It provides ***flexibility*** by supporting interoperability between different system, device or protocol
- It is ***scalable*** because the push model of information transfer used in XMPP solves serious scaling problems associated with traditional HTTP-based polling approaches
- It is ***extensible*** because it has a technology for rapid delivery of XML from one place to another. It has also been used for a wide range of applications

Applications

- Video
- File transfer
- Gaming
- Signalling for VoIP
- Gaming
- Social networking
- Alerts and Notifications
- Geolocation Application
- Intelligent workflows
- Machine-to-Machine communication

5. Data Distribution Service (DDS)

Data Distribution Service is an IoT protocol designed for real-time machine to machine or device to device communication. It was developed by the Object Management Group (OMG) and it standardises the software Application Programming interface. It follows publish-subscribe methodology to enable scalable, real-time, dependable, high-performance and interoperable data exchange. The publisher creates topic to which aubscribers can subscribe to it. As compared to MQTT and CoAP protocols, DDS makes use of brokerless architecture and multicasting to bring good quality of QoS to applications. DDS can be deployed in platforms ranging from low-footprint devices to the cloud. The DDS protocol has two main layers:

- ✯ Data Centric Publish-Subscribe (DCPS): performs the task of delivering the information to subscribers
- ✯ Data-Local Reconstruction Layer (DLRL): Provides an interface to DCPS functionalities, enabling the sharing of distributed data among IoT enabled objects

DDS Entities

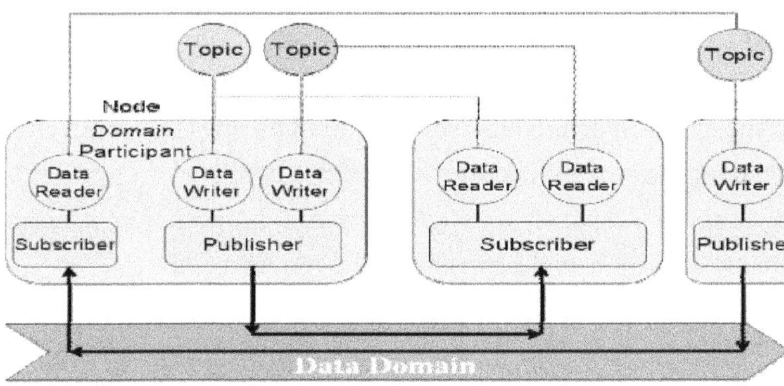

DDS Entities

The data is sent and received from the data domain. The Publishers and the Subscribers are used to manage single or multiple Data Writers and Data Readers. A Data Reader and Data Writer must be associated to the same Topic if data published by the Data Writer is to be received by the subscribing Data Reader.

Advantages of DDS

Based on a simple *"publish-subscribe"* communication paradigm

- ✯ Flexible and adaptable architecture that supports "auto-discovery" of new or stale endpoint applications
- ✯ Less overhead—can be used with high-performance systems
- ✯ Deterministic data delivery
- ✯ Dynamically scalable
- ✯ Efficient use of transport bandwidth
- ✯ Supports one-to-one, one-to-many, many-to-one, and many-to-many communications
- ✯ Large number of configuration parameters that give developers complete control of each message in the system

6. Constrained Application Protocol (CoAP)

CoAP is used for web transfer in resource constrained network (limited energy, power, resources, *etc*,). It is equivalent to HTTP. It is a session layer protocol and also contributes as an Application layer protocol. CoAP web-objects communicate using Request- Response interaction model. It uses object-model for the resources and each object can have single or multiple instances. Each resource can have single or multiple instances. It works on the top of UDP (where TCP for HTTP). The client-server interaction is Asynchronous. REST (Representation State Transfer) is the standard interface between HTTP clients and servers. It is a resource hungry protocol and so it is not good for IoT. CoAP is designed to enable low power sensors to use RESTful services while meeting their power constraints. The access by a CoAP object or itsr resource is thus using:

- URI
- A subset of MIME types
- A subset of response codes which are used for an HTTP object or resource.

CoAP architecture is divided into two main sub-layers:

- **Messaging:** Responsible for reliability and duplication of message
- **Request/Response:** Responsible for communication

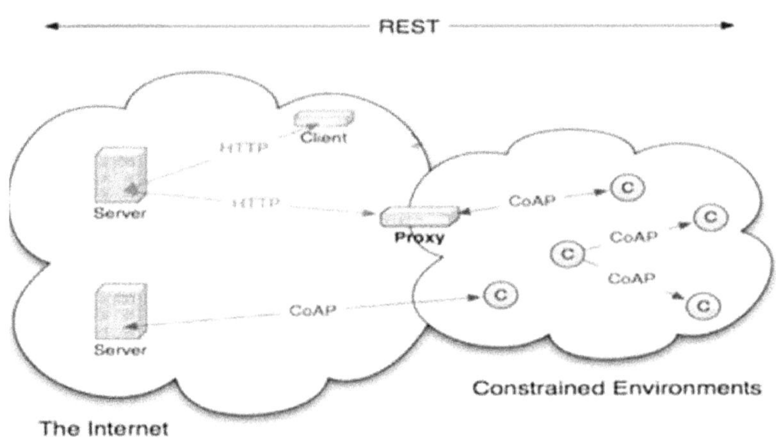

CoAP Architecture

CoAP has four messaging modes:

- Confirmable
- Non-Confirmable
- Piggyback
- Separate

Features

1. Reduced overheads and parsing complexity
2. URL and content-type support
3. Support for discovery of resources provided by known CoAP services
4. Simple subscription for resources and resulting push notification
5. Simple caching based on maximum message

4. IoT Communication Models

The IoT communication model provides information about how IoT devices can be connected and communicated.

1. Intelligent Device-to-Device Communication

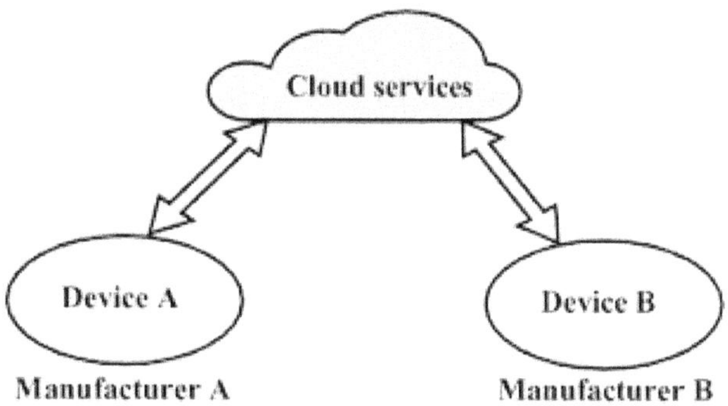

Device-to-device communication model represents direct communication between two or more devices rather than intermediary application server. In IoT ecosystem the devices are the main users. Device-to-device communication is expected to be an intrinsic part of the IoT. Device will communicate with each other autonomously without any centralised control and collaborate to gather, share and forward information in a multihop manner. The devices communicate over different types of network. The devices use protocol like Blue tooth, Zigbee, Z-wave to establish device to device communication. The ability to gather relevant information in real time is a key to leverage the value of IoT since such information will be transformed into intelligence which will facilitate the creation of intelligent environment.

Problems in Device to Device communication:

- ✯ Sensitive information disclosure
- ✯ DoS attack
- ✯ Buffer overflow attack
- ✯ Stealing of Authentication credential
- ✯ Improper updation of firmware

2. Device-to-Cloud Communication

Device to cloud communication model represents communication between device and cloud service provider for exchange of data and control message traffic. This approach makes use of existing communications mechanism such as wired Ethernet or WiFi connections to establish connection between device and the cloud service provider. The cloud connection enables the user to obtain remote access through smart phone or Web interface. The device to cloud model adds value to the end user by extending the capabilities of the devices beyond its native features. The integration of devices from different manufacturers can lead to interoperability challenges. The device and cloud service are mostly from the same vendor. When sending information from the application in the device to the solution back end, IoT Hub exposes three options:

i. Device-to-cloud messages for time series telemetry and alerts

ii. Device twin's reported properties for reporting device state information such as available capabilities, conditions or the state of long running workflows

iii. File uploads for media files and large telemetry batches upload by intermittently connected devices or compressed to save bandwidth

IoT hub provides three options for device application to expose functionality to a back-end application:

i. Direct methods for communications that require intermediate confirmation of the result. Direct methods are often used to interactive control of devices such as turning on a fan

ii. Twin's desired properties for long-running commands intended to put the device into desired state.

iii. Cloud to device messages for one way notifications to the device application

Problems in Device to Device communication:

- SQL injection, cross-site scripting attack
- Man in the middle attack
- Username and password enumeration attack
- Cross site request forgery on cloud application interfaces

3. Device-to-Gateway Communication

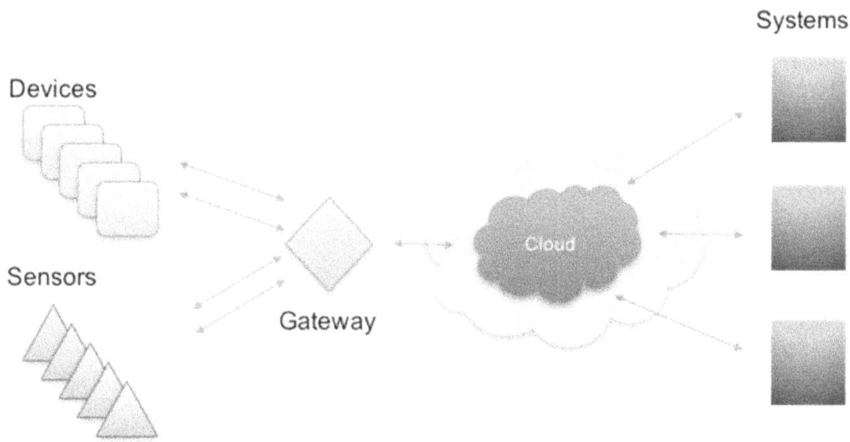

In the device to gateway model, the IoT device connects through an Application Layer Gateway to communicate with cloud service provider. The devices that don't have ability to connect directly to a cloud service rely on gateway for their communication. So, the gateway acts as an intermediary between the device and the cloud service. IoT gateways sit at the junction of edge systems such as devices, controllers, sensors and the cloud. The hub device in home automation is the gateway. The gateway provides several critical functions such as device connectivity, security, data or protocol translation, data filtering and processing and more. The data moving to the cloud or vice-versa goes through the gateway. It can be either a dedicated hardware appliance or software program. The local gateway device can also be a smart phone running an application to communicate with a device and cloud service provider. IoT gateways need to support the following functionality:

- ✯ Trusted Connectivity and Security: Ensuring the integrity of the network and system
- ✯ Protocol and Data Bridge: Being able to transfer data among and between systems operating with different communications protocols and data formats
- ✯ Storage and Analysis: Onboard application development platforms and storage to drive intelligence and decision making closer to the device
- ✯ Management: The ability to provision, update and control access of devices to the system as well as policy-based permissions

4. Data Sharing Model

IoT is the most significant sources of new data and the data science will provide a considerable contribution in making IoT applications more intelligent. The back-end data sharing model provides Application Programming Interfaces (APIs) for achieving interoperability of smart device. The data sharing model refers to a communication architecture that enables the user to export and analyse the smart device data from a cloud service in combination with data from other sources. Data science is the combination of data mining, machine learning and other techniques to find the insight from the data. These techniques include a broad range of algorithms applicable in different domains. The process of applying data analytics methods to a particular area involves defining data types (volume, variety and velocity), data models (Neural networks, classification and clustering) and applying efficient algorithms that match with the data characteristics. The following are the steps to be followed

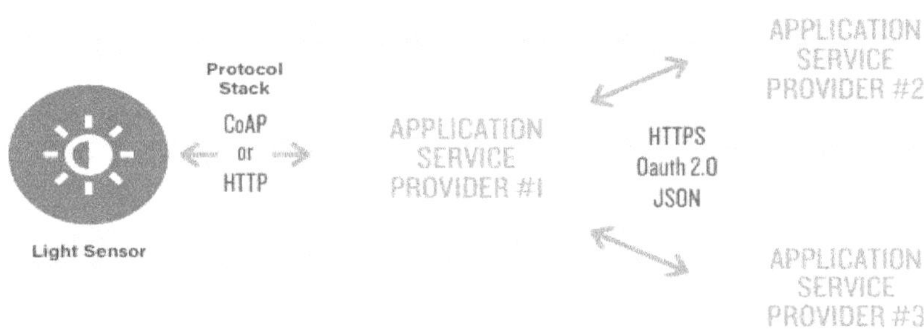

- ★ Since data is generated from different sources with varying datatypes, it is important to develop algorithm that can handle the data characteristics
- ★ Large number of resources that generate data in real time are known without the problem of scale and velocity
- ★ Finding the best data model that fits the data is one of the most important issues for pattern recognition and for better analysis of IoT data

IoT Communication APIs

The two communication APIs are

- ★ REST-based communication APIs
- ★ Web-socket based communication APIs

REST-based Communication APIs

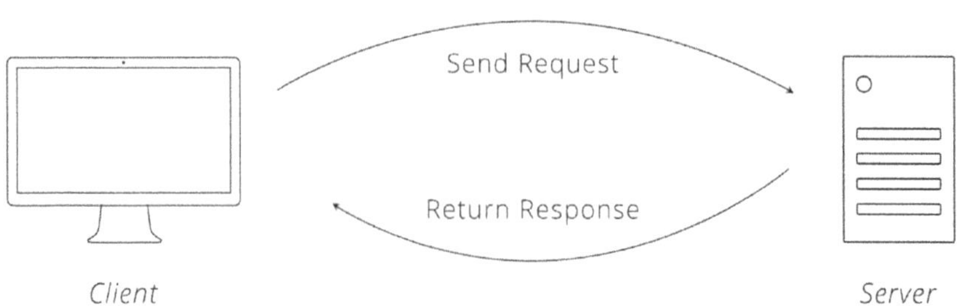

REST (Representation State Transfer) is a set of architectural principles to design web services and web APIs that focus on a system resources and how resource states are addressed and transferred. REST APIs follow *request-response* communication model. (Request –Response is a communication model in which the client sends requests to the server and the server responds to the request). A RESTful web service is a web API implemented using HTTP and REST principles. The various HTTP methods are

- GET
- POST
- PUT
- DELETE

Web-Socket based Communication APIs

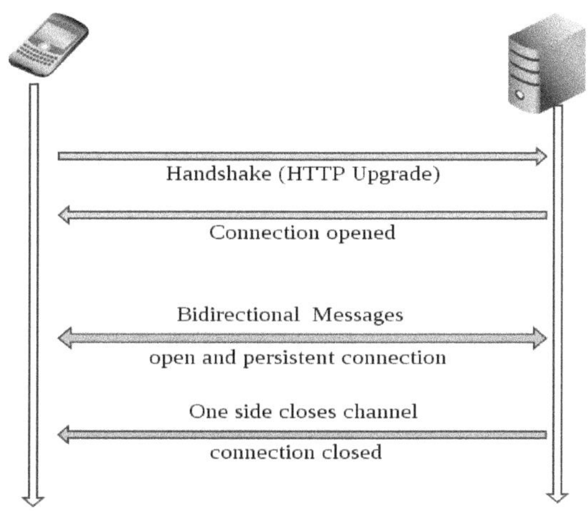

Web-Socket APIs allows bidirectional, full duplex communication between clients and servers. It follows the *exclusive pair* communication model. (Exclusive pair communication model is a bi-directional, fully duplex communication model that uses a persistent connection between client and server). Web-Socket communication begins with a connection setup request sent by client to the server. If the server supports WebSocket protocol, the server responds to the WebSocket handshake response. After the connection is established, the client and server send data or message to each other in full-duplex mode. The advantages of Websocket APIs

- Reduces network traffic and latency
- No overhead for connection setup
- Low latency
- High thoroughput

5. IoT Enabling Technologies

The following entities provide a diverse technology-environment and are involved in IoT. The entities are

- Hardware (Arduino, Raspberry pi, Intel Edison, *etc.,*)
- Integrated Development Environment
- Protocols (RPL, CoAP, RESTful, HTTP, *etc.,*)
- Communication (RFID, NFC, Zigbee, Bluetooth, WIFI, *etc.,*)
- Network Backbone (IPv4, IPv6,UDP,etc.,)
- Software (Contiki OS, Thingsquare, *etc.,*)
- Internetwork cloud platform/Data Centre
- Machine Learning Algorithm and Software

The following section provides an overview of the technologies that play a key-role in IoT:

1. Wireless Sensor Network
2. Cloud Computing
3. Big Data Analytics
4. Communication Protocol
5. Embedded System

1. Wireless Sensor Network

A Wireless Sensor Network is a self-configuring, infrastructureless, low cost, application oriented network of small distributed sensor nodes communicating among themselves using radio signals. It is deployed in quantity to sense, monitor and understand the physical world. Wireless Sensor nodes are called *motes*. WSN provide a bridge between the real physical and virtual worlds. It has a wide range of potential applications to industry, science, transportation, civil infrastructure and security. The design of WSN becomes more complex due to characteristics of deploying nodes, security, authentication and its scenario of operation.

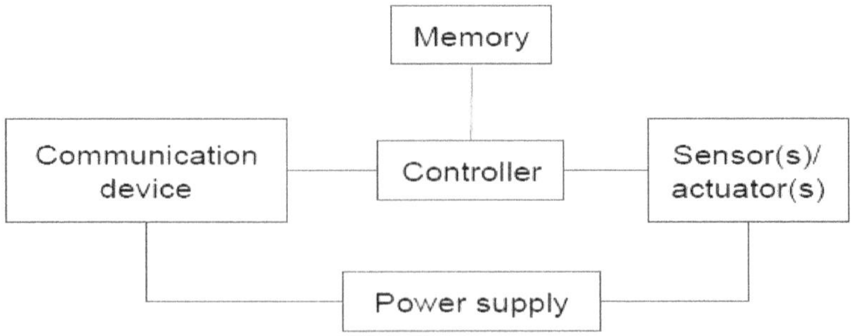

Components of Mote

Applications of Wireless Sensor Networks

1. Agriculture

Environmental applications include tracking the movements and patterns of insects, birds or small animals. It is also used to monitor the humidity condition of the soil.

2. Structural Monitoring

Wireless sensors can be used to monitor the movements in the buildings and infrastructure such as bridges, flyovers, embankments, tunnels *etc.* It enables to monitor assets remotely without the need for site visits. The data are collected daily, whereas traditionally this data was collected weekly or monthly, using physical site visits, involving either road or rail closure in some cases. It is far more accurate than any visual inspection that would be carried out.

3. Industrial Process Control

In Industry, WSNs can be used for monitoring the manufacturing process or the condition and controlling of manufacturing equipment. For example, in oil refineries sensors are used to monitor the condition of their miles of pipelines. These sensors are used to alert in case of any failures or damages occurred.

4. Military or Border Surveillance Application

WSN is becoming an integral part of military for communication (commanding), control and intelligence systems. Sensors can be deployed in a battle field to monitor the presence of vehicles and to track their movements, enabling close surveillance of opposing forces.

5. Healthcare Applications

Wireless sensor networks can be used to monitor and track elders and patients for health care purposes, which can significantly relieve the severe shortage of health care personnel and reduce the health care expenditures in the current health care systems. For example sensors can be deployed in a patient's home to monitor the behaviours of the patient. It can alert doctors when the patient falls and requires immediate medical attention.

2. Cloud Computing

Cloud computing is a combination of parallel and distributed computing and various technologies. Cloud applications are data intensive applications and computation can also be done on the cloud. Many concurrent machines can run parallel in the cloud. An acquisition and delivery model of IT resources helps in the Business performance improvement and controls the cost of IT-delivering resources to the organisation. The two perspectives of cloud computing are

- User perspective: User need not worry about how and who is taking care of all the offered services. Users use all the services over the Internet using the Web browser. There is a full layer of abstraction and invisibility from the user point of view

* Organisation perspective: Cloud delivers services for consumer and business needs in a simple way. It provides on-demand scalability and distinguished QoS to increase rapid innovation and decision making in the business rather than focusing on the infrastructure need and complexity

The services offered by Cloud Computing are

1. Infrastructure-as-a-Service (IaaS)
2. Platform-as-a-Service (PaaS)
3. Software-as-a-Service (SaaS)

Infrastructure-as-a-Service

IaaS provides the users the ability to provision computing and storage resources. The resources are provided to the users as virtual machine instances and virtual storage. Users can start, stop, configure and manage the virtual machine instances and virtual storage. The cloud service providers manage the underlying infrastructure. Virtual resources provisioned by the users are billed based on pay-per-use paradigm.

Some of the infrastructure providers are

* Amazon Web Services
* Rackspace Cloud
* Google compute Engine
* Microsoft Azure Services
* GoGrid

Platform as a Service

PaaS is a computing platform, offered through the Web. Web applications can be created and codes can be deployed without purchasing any license software or hardware. PaaS offerings are specific to Web developers, Web designers and application developers. The consumer does not manage or control the underlying cloud infrastructure including network, servers, operating systems or storage but has control over the deployed applications and possibly application hosting environment configurations.

Some PaaS providers and the environments they provide are as follows:

* Microsoft's Azure
* Google's App Engine
* Salesfore.com's Force.com
* VM Ware's Cloud Foundry
* Engine Yard

Software as a Service

SaaS provides the user a complete software application or the user interface to the application itself. SaaS applications are platform independent and can be accessed by various client devices such as workstation, laptop, tablets and smartphones. Various advanced and traditional applications come under SaaS. The SaaS providers develop applications according to current market demands and customer requirements. SaaS-based applications are generally preferred by all Internet and computer users.

Some SaaS providers are:

- icloud.com
- Mint.com
- eyeOS
- Cloudo

Virtual Machine

A Virtual machine is a closely detached software device that could run its own operating systems (OS) and applications as if it is running on a physical computer. A VM works like a physical computer and contains its own virtual RAM, hard disk, CPU and netrwork interface card.

3. Big Data Analytics

Big data is data that is huge in volume, velocity and variety. Big data is data whose scale, distribution, diversity and/or timeliness require the use of analytics to enable insights that unlock new sources of business value.

Drivers of Big Data

- Medical information
- Photos and videos uploaded to the World Wide Web
- Video Surveillance
- Mobile devices
- Smart devices
- Non traditional IT devices

i. Volume

The quantity of data generated in the world has been doubling every year. It grows from bits to bytes to petabytes and exabytes

Bits->Bytes->Kilobytes->Megabytes->Gigabytes->Terabytes->Petabytes->Exabytes-> Zettabytes->Yottabytes

The growth of data is given by

Bits	0 or 1
Bytes	8 bits
Kilobytes	1024 bytes
Megabytes	$(1024)^2$ bytes

Gigabytes	$(1024)^3$ bytes
Terabytes	$(1024)^4$ bytes
Petabytes	$(1024)^5$ bytes
Exabytes	$(1024)^6$ bytes
Zettabytes	$(1024)^7$ bytes
Yottabytes	$(1024)^8$ bytes

The reason for the growth of data is the dramatic reduction in the cost of storing data. The cost of computation and communication of data have also come down.

ii. Velocity

Velocity refers to the rate at which the data are generated. Big Data is generated by billions of devices and communicated through the Internet. The primary reason for the increased velocity of the data is the increase in Internet speed.

iii. Variety

Variety deals with a wide range of data types and sources of data. The three categories of data are

- **Structured data:** Data containing a defined data type, format and structure are called structured data

  E.g. RDBMS, Spread-sheets

- **Semi-structured data:** Textual data files with a discernible pattern that enables parsing

  E.g. XML schema

- **Unstructured data:** Data that has no inherent structure which may include text documents, PDFs, images and video

4. Communication Protocols

Communication protocols allow devices to exchange data over the network. It enables network connectivity and coupling to applications. It forms the backbone of the IoT systems. The functions of the protocol include

- Data sequencing
- Data Routing
- Flow control
- Error control
- Retransmission of lost packets

5. Embedded Systems

Embedded systems include an application specific Integrated circuit or micro-controller to perform a specific dedicated application. Embedded systems are pre-programmed to do specific functions. The Embedded processor co-ordinates with the rest of the components to achieve the overall functions. It embeds a real time operating system (RTOS) which supervises the application software task running on the hardware and organises the access to system resources according to priorities and timing constraints of tasks in the system. Embedded RTOS enables execution of concurrent task, process or threads. The characteristics of embedded systems are

- ★ Dedicated function
- ★ Dedicated complex algorithm
- ★ Dedicated GUIs and other user interfaces for the application
- ★ Real time operations
- ★ Multi rate operations

5. IoT LEVELS

The Internet of Things has enhanced the companies by giving more reach and features to build the advanced products. This trend goes beyond IT and manufacturing companies. There are numerous ways that industries can leverage their IoT technologies. There are four level of IoT implementation. They are

- ★ Meaurement
- ★ Automation
- ★ Innovation
- ★ Cloud Storage and Analysis

Level 1: Measurement

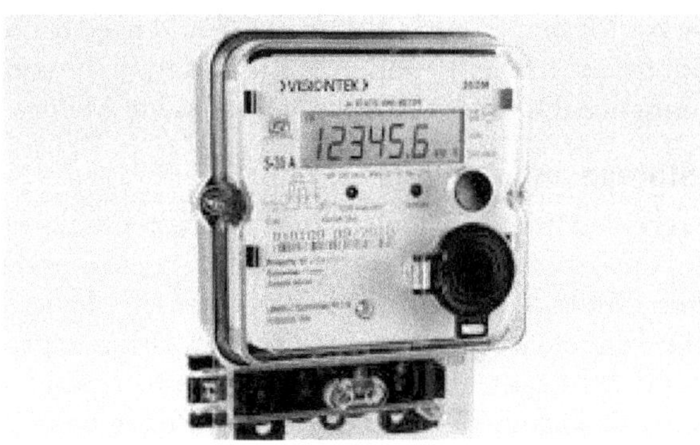

In this level, IoT is simply used to record data and do nothing more than that. It does not trigger any succeeding event. It is the most basic level of implementation. The measurement based IoT devices are being used by the Governments to measure and transmit real-time data from street lights, traffic cameras and other deployments to a central system.

e.g. Electricity Meter. It exists to take note of how much electricity is being consumed but does not alert if certain amount of electricity is used

Level 2: Automation

In this level, IoT devices not just record data but also execute automated business process. In Automation, business must first decide their part of operation or process that needs the aggregated data and then identify how to process and use the information.

E.g. Electricity Meter with automation: Electricity meter would send the automated SMS alert to the consumers with details regarding their consumption of energy

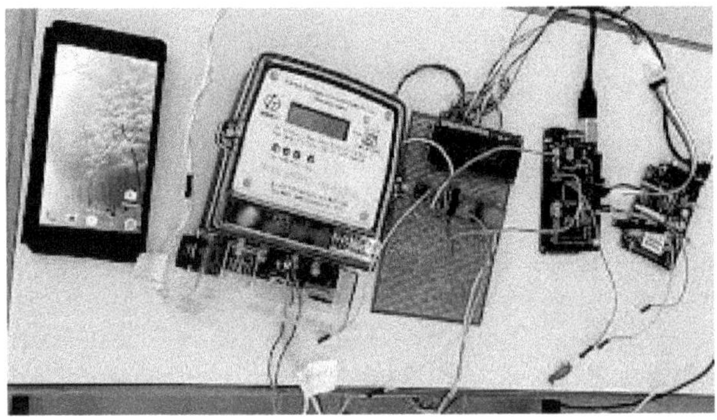

Level 3: Innovation

In this level, IoT lends itself to innovation quickly and easily. Manufacturers integrate IoT into their products and can make them more attractive to buyers. The important thing here is for the Business to collaborate with the third party hardware and software developers in the IoT deployment process.

Example: Electric Motors- The manufacturer would need to collaborate with an electronic provider for the implementation of IoT and with the software developers to build apps to enhance the functionality of IoT-enabled Meters

Level 4: Cloud Storage and Analysis

The data are received from IoT devices and stored on the cloud. The services are provided by using the data that lives on the cloud. The users and stakeholders can access the data from anywhere and from any device. The devices use the Internet to transmit real-time data to a central server, uses algorithm to process and analyse the information and then take automated decisions to change the way the end devices work. Many Governments across the world have been planning a future where public utilities are IoT-enabled in such a way that the resources consumed by them are optimized in real-time.

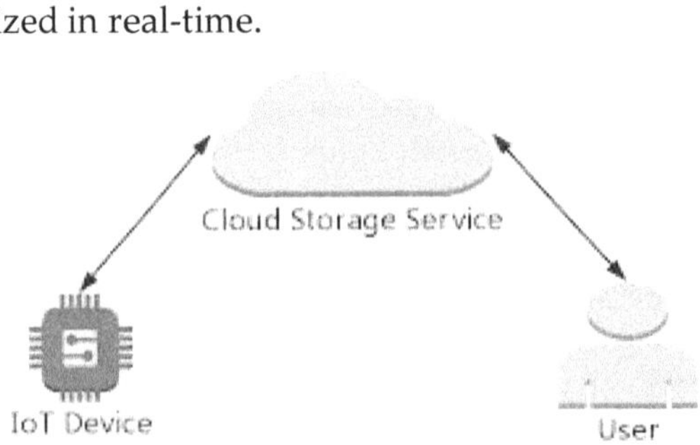

Example: Traffic Intersection changes the duration of a signal depending on real time traffic condition.

The advantage is that it is quite easy to move up from one level to the next. For instance if there is all the data to automate the distribution chain then use the same IoT system to deliver more service to the customers such as real time order fulfillment or order tracking.

6. Domain Specific IoTs

IoT provides many applications in human life, making life easier, safe and smart. There are many applications such as

- ✯ Smart Cities
- ✯ Smart Home and Buildings
- ✯ Smart Transportation
- ✯ Smart Energy and Grid
- ✯ Smart Environment

Smart Cities

Smart cities are the cities of the smart life. The cities can be improved in many levels by using IoT. They are

- ✯ Improving infrastructure
- ✯ Enhancing public transportation reducing traffic congestion
- ✯ Keeping cities safe and healthy
- ✯ More engaged in the community

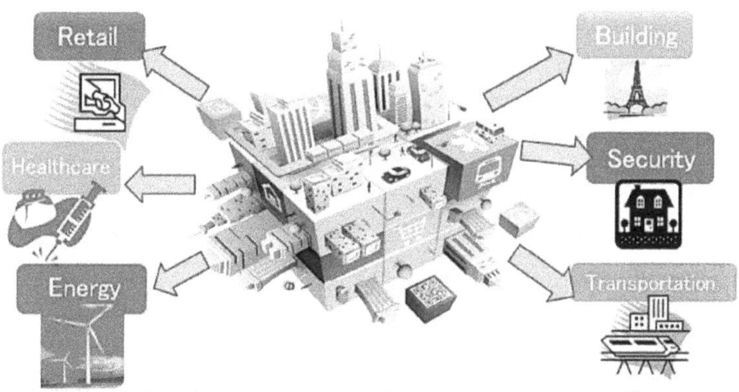

Smart Home and Buildings

By the concept of IoT, homes and buildings may operate many devices and objects smartly. The smart applications of IoT in smart homes and buildings are

- ✯ Smart lighting
- ✯ Smart environmental and media air control

- ★ Central heating
- ★ Energy management and
- ★ Security

Many companies are developing platforms that integrate the building automation with entertainment, healthcare monitoring, energy monitoring and wireless sensor monitoring in the home and building environments. The mobile devices ensure that consumer have access to portable controller for the electronics connected to the network. Wi-Fi technologies in the home automation are used for the networked nature of electronic devices such as TVs, mobile devices, *etc.*, are usually supported by Wi-Fi.

Smart Transportation

The innovation in transportation is one of the factors to indicate the prosperous of the country. The most important of IoT transformation application are

- ★ Alert applications of traffic
- ★ Transportation control (Routing of vehicles + Speed control+ Transportation control)
- ★ Vehicle connectivity and
- ★ Road condition monitoring

Smart Energy and Grid

A smart grid is developed for smart energy management. Today's grid is reliable with normal electricity fluctuations. It allows integration of renewable energy and green technologies to offer many benefits to customer in cost savings through efficient energy use at home. The smart grid that incorporates ICTs (Information and communication technologies) to the network of electricity will enable a two way communication between suppliers and consumers, creates more dynamic interaction on energy flow and deliver electricity more efficiently and sustainably. The elements of information and communications technologies include

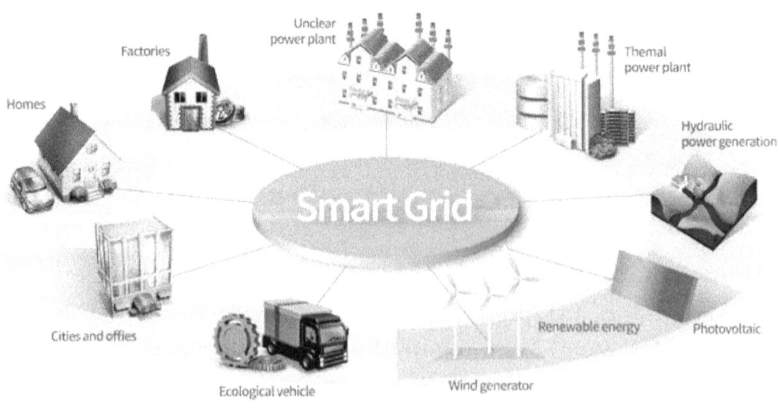

- ★ Sensing and monitoring technologies for power flows

- Digital communication infrastructure to transmit data across the grid
- Smart meters (Inform usage, coordination, control)
- Co-ordination control
- Automation System (To aggregate and process data)
- Interactive and responsive electricity

Smart Environment

Environment plays a major role in human life. Living beings are affected by unhealthy environment. The environment needs a smart ways and technologies for monitoring and management. Monitoring and waste management provide a large amount of data for the healthy environment and organisations. It protects people and environment by mitigating or avoiding natural disaster that might occur. The IoT applications can be divided into two main categories

- Environmental resource management
- Environment quality and protection management

IoT can provide an efficient way to communicate between natural resources like animals, planets, birds, *etc.* The IoT technology also monitors and manages the air quality by collecting data from remote sensor across the city. The IoT can be used to measure the pollution levels in water in order to inform decisions on water usage and treatment. IoT provides an environmental protection by the control of industrial pollution by means of real time monitoring and management. The systems are integrated to supervision and decision making networks to reduce waste and improve environment.

The other aspect is a weather forecasting and monitoring. IoT provides high resolution and accuracy for weather monitoring by data exchange and information sharing. IoT helps in collecting weather data from sensors which are stored in cloud for analysis. *Radiation* is one of the most serious problems threatening the safety of the environment. The radiation control IoT sensor network is able to continuously monitor the radiation levels around nuclear facilities for leakage detection and propagation prevention.

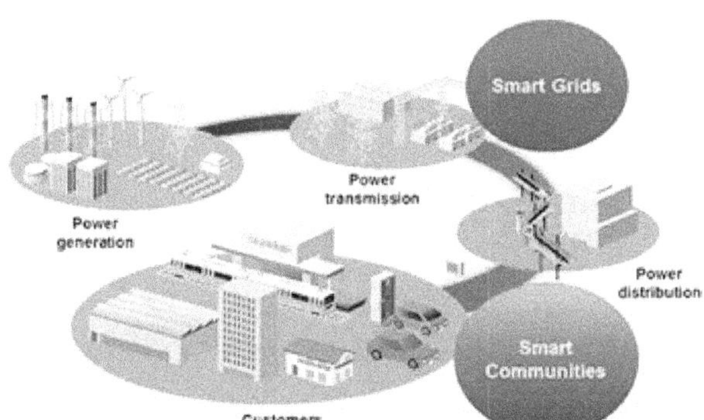

7. IoT Vs M2M

M2M

M2M allows communication between devices of the same type and a specific application via wired or wireless networks. M2M refers to networking of machines for the purpose of remote monitoring and control of enterprise assets or to provide connectivity of remote machine type. Remote monitoring is an incentive for industrial applications. M2M solutions allow end-users to capture data about events from assets. It is deployed to increase safety/security, productivity gains and reduce costs. M2M don't allow for the broad sharing of data or connection of the devices directly to the Internet.

Key Features of M2M

The key features of M2M system are given below:

1. **Low Mobility** : M2M Devices do not move, move infrequently, or move only within a certain region
2. **Controlled** : Send or receive data only at certain pre-defined periods
3. **Time Tolerant** : Data transfer can be delayed
4. **Packet Switched** : Network operator to provide packet switched service with or without an MSISDN
5. **Online small Data Transmissions**: MTC Devices frequently send or receive small amounts of data.
6. **Monitoring**: Not intend to prevent theft or vandalism but provide functionality to detect the events
7. **Low Power Consumption** : To improve the ability of the system to efficiently service M2M applications
8. **Location Specific Trigger** : Intending to trigger M2M device in a particular area *e.g.* wake up the device

M2M Value Chain

A value chain describes the full range of activities that firms and workers perform to bring a product from its conception to end use and beyond, including

- ✯ Design
- ✯ Production
- ✯ Marketing
- ✯ Distribution and
- ✯ Support to the final consumer

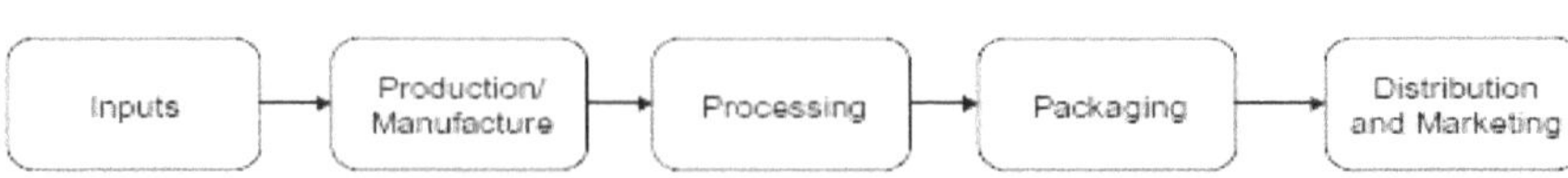

Simplified global value chain

Inputs

Inputs are the base raw ingredients that are turned into a product.

Example: Data from an M2M device that will be turned into a piece of information.

Production/Manufacture

Production/Manufacture refers to the process that the raw inputs are put through to become part of a value chain.

Example: Data from an M2M solution needs to be verified and tagged for provenance.

Processing

Processing refers to the process whereby a product is prepared for sale.

Example: In M2M solution, processing refers to the aggregation of multiple data sources to create an information component i.e, something that is ready to be combined with other data sets to make it useful for corporate *decision-making*.

Packaging

Packaging refers to the process whereby a product can be branded as would be recognizable to end-user consumers.

Example: The data have to be combined with other information from internal corporate databases. This data would be recognizable to the end-users that need to use the information either in the form of visualizations or an Excel spreadsheet.

Distribution/Marketing

This process refers to the channels to market for products. Information Product can be used to create new knowledge within a corporate environment.

Example: More detailed scheduling of maintenance based on real-world information or improved product design due to feedback from the M2M solution

IoT Value Chain

Inputs

The first is that there are significantly many inputs for IoT compared to M2M. The input devices are

- Devices/Sensors
- Open Data
- OSS/BSS
- Corporate Databases

i. Devices/Sensors

In M2M, devices and sensors are built on the same technology. But devices and sensors used in IoT may or may not be on the same technology but provides a different and much broader marketplace than M2M does

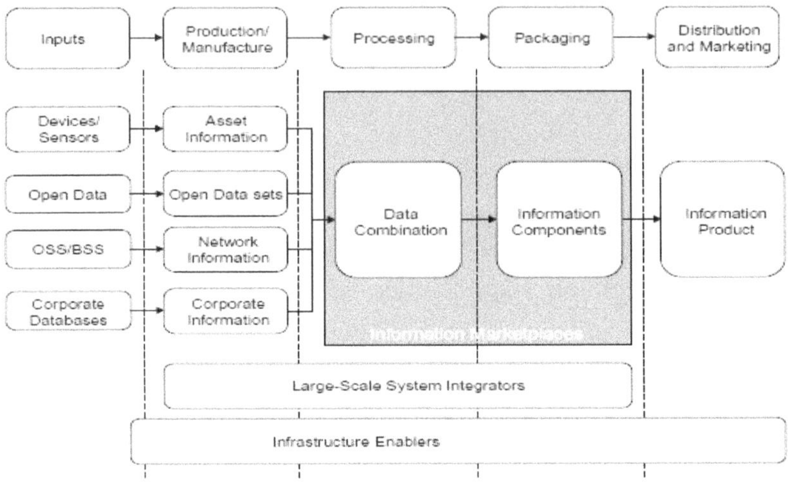

ii. Open Data

Open data is an important input to Information Value Chains. Open Data is defined as a piece of data that is free to use, reuse, and redistribute. Open data requires a license stating that it is open data.

Example: City maps provided by organizations such as Ordinance Survey

iii. OSS/BSS

The *Operational Support Systems* and *Business Support Systems* of mobile operator networks are also important inputs to information value chains, and are being used increasingly in tightly closed information marketplaces that allow operators to deliver services to Enterprises

iv. Corporate Databases

Companies of a certain size generally have multiple corporate databases covering various functions, including supply chain management, payroll, accounting, *etc.* As the use of devices and sensors increases, these databases will be connected to this data to create new information sources and new knowledge.

Production/Manufacture

In the production and manufacturing processes for data in an IoT solution, the raw inputs undergo initial development into information components and products. Irrespective of type of input described above, this process will need to include *tagging and linking of relevant data items* in order to provide provenance and traceability across the information value chain.

i. Asset Information

Asset information may include data such as temperature over time of container during transit or air quality during a particular month. Essentially, this relates to whatever the sensor/device has been developed to monitor.

ii. Open Data Sets

Open data sets may include maps, rail timetables, or demographics about a certain area in a country or city.

iii. Network Information

Network information relates to information such as GPS data, services accessed via the mobile network, *etc.* . . .

iii. Corporate Information: Corporate information may be, for example, the current state of demand for a particular product in the supply chain at a particular moment in time.

Processing

During the processing stage, data from various sources is mixed together. At this point, the data from the various inputs from the production and manufacture stage are combined together to create information. This process involves the extensive use of data analytics for M2M and IoT solutions

Packaging

After the data from various inputs has been combined together, the packaging section of the information value chain creates information components. These components could be produced as *charts* or other traditional methods of communicating information to end-users.

Both the processing and packaging sections of the Information-Driven Global Value Chain (I-GVC) are where Information Marketplaces will be developed. At this point, data sets with appropriate *data tagging and traceability* could be exchanged with other economic actors for feeding into their own information product development processes. Alternatively, a Market Perspective company may instead select to exchange information components, which represent a higher level of data abstraction of their corporate information.

Distribution/Marketing

The final stage of the Information Value Chain is the creation of an Information Product. A broad variety of such products may exist, but they fall into two main categories:

i. **Information products for improving internal decision-making:** These information products are the result of either detailed information analysis that allows better decisions to be made during various internal corporate processes or they enable the creation of previously unavailable knowledge about a company's products, strategy or internal processes.

ii. **Information products for resale to other economic actors:** These information products have high value for other economic actors and can be sold to them.

For example, through an IoT solution, a company may have market information about a certain area of town that another entity might pay for (*e.g.* a real-estate company).

M2M Components

M2M system consists of

- ★ M2M devices
- ★ Network
- ★ M2M service Enablement
- ★ M2M application

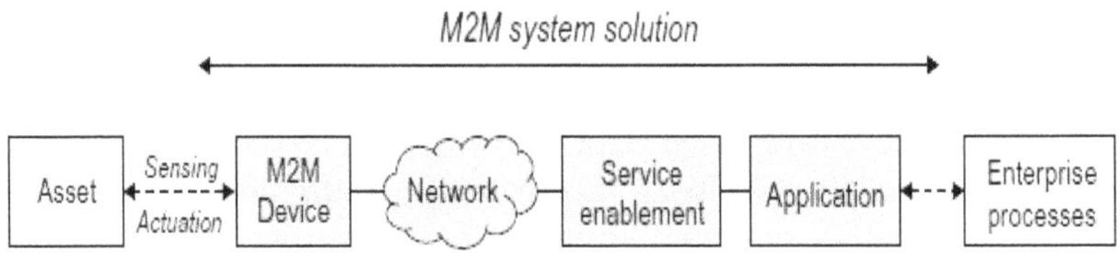

A Generic M2M solution

M2M Device

Sensor and communication devices are the endpoints of M2M applications. It provides sensing and actuation capabilities. These devices can be from low-end sensor nodes to high-end complex devices with multimodal sensing capabilities. Devices can connect directly to an operator's network or interconnect using WPAN technologies such as Bluetooth or ZigBee. Addressing and identifying of the devices relies heavily on the gateways. Devices that connect via gateways are normally outside the network's responsibility but belong to M2M applications that are provided by application or service providers. The devices and sensors that connect directly to an operator's network are endpoints of the network.

Network

The objective of the network is to provide remote connectivity between the M2M device and the application-side servers. Different types of network can be used. It also includes Local Area Networks and Wide Area Networks. Examples of WANs are public cellular networks, fixed private networks or even satellite links.

M2M Service Enablement

This provides generic functionality that is common across a number of different applications. The ultimate aim of this component is to reduce the implementation cost and ease of application development.

M2M Application

The application component is used to monitor and control process. The application is integrated into overall business process. The process of monitoring and controlling the assets remotely can be of different types. It contains the middleware layer where data goes through various application services and is used by the specific business-processing engines. Applications may either target at end users or at other application providers to offer more refined building blocks by which they can build more M2M solutions and services

Requirements of M2M

The general requirements for the M2M system are given below:

1. M2M Application Communication Principles

The M2M system allows communication between M2M Applications in the Network and Applications Domain, the M2M Device or M2M Gateway by using multiple communication means, *e.g.* SMS, GPRS and IP Access. A Connected Object may be able to communicate in a peer-to-peer manner with any other Connected Object. The M2M System should abstract the underlying network structure including any network addressing mechanism used, *e.g.* in case of an IP based network the session establishment shall be possible when IP static or dynamic addressing is used.

2. Message Delivery for Sleeping Devices

The M2M System manages communication towards a sleeping device.

3. Delivery Modes

The M2M System shall support

- *Anycast
- *Unicast
- *Multicast and
- *Broadcast communication modes.

Whenever possible a global broadcast should be replaced by an anycast or multicast in order to minimize the load on the communication network.

4. Message Transmission Scheduling

The M2M System manages the scheduling of network access and messaging. It will be aware of the scheduling delay tolerance of the M2M Application.

5. Message Communication Path Selection

The M2M System optimizes the communication paths, based on policies such as

- Network cost
- Delays or
- Transmission failures when other communication paths exist.

6. Communication with Devices behind a M2M Gateway

The M2M System should be able to communicate with Devices behind a M2M gateway.

7. Communication Failure Notification

M2M Applications which request the reliable delivery of a message will be notified of any failures to deliver the message.

8. Scalability

The M2M System will be scalable in terms of number of Connected Objects.

9. Abstraction of Technologies Heterogeneity

The M2M Gateway is capable of interfacing with various M2M Area Network technologies.

10. M2M Service Capabilities Discovery and Registration

The M2M System supports mechanisms to allow M2M Applications to discover M2M service capabilities offered to them. The M2M Device and M2M Gateway also support mechanisms to allow the registration of its M2M Service Capabilities to the M2M system.

11. M2M Trusted Application

The M2M Core handles the service request responses for trusted M2M Applications by allowing streamlined authentication procedures for these applications. The M2M system may support trusted applications that are pre-validated by the M2M Core.

12. Mobility

If the underlying network supports seamless mobility and roaming, the M2M System will use such mechanisms.

13. Communications Integrity

The M2M System support mechanisms to assure communications integrity for M2M services.

14. Device/Gateway Integrity Check

The M2M System shall support M2M Device and M2M Gateway integrity check.

15. Continuous Connectivity

The M2M System supports continuous connectivity for M2M applications requesting the same M2M service on a regular and continuous basis. This continuous connectivity may be de-activated upon request of the Application or by an internal mechanism in the M2M Core.

16. Confirm

The M2M System will support mechanisms to confirm messages. A message will be unconfirmed, confirmed or transaction controlled.

17. Priority

The M2M System supports the management of priority levels of the services and communications services. Ongoing communications may be interrupted in order to serve a flow with higher priority (*i.e.* pre-emption).

18. Logging

Messaging and transactions requiring non-repudiation will be capable of being logged. Important events (*e.g.* received information from the M2M Device or M2M Gateway is faulty, unsuccessful installation attempt from the M2M Device or M2M Gateway, service not operating, *etc.*) will be logged together with diagnostic information. Logs can be retrievable upon request.

19. Anonymity

The M2M System supports Anonymity. If anonymity is requested by an M2M Application from the M2M Device side and the request is accepted by the network, the network infrastructure will hide the identity and the location of the requestor, subject to regulatory requirements.

20. Time Stamp

The M2M System supports accurate, secure and trusted time stamping. M2M Devices and M2M Gateways will support accurate, secure and trusted time stamping.

21. Device/Gateway Failure Robustness

After a non-destructive failure, *e.g.* after a power supply outage, a M2M Device or Gateway should immediately return in a full operating state autonomously, after performing the appropriate initialization

e.g. Integrity check if supported.

22. Radio Transmission Activity Indication and Control

The radio transmitting parts (*e.g.* GSM/GPRS) of the M2M Device/Gateway will provide a real-time indication of radio transmission activity to the application on the M2M Device/Gateway, and will be instructed real-time by the application on the M2M Device/Gateway to suspend/resume the radio transmission activity.

Applications of M2M

The applications of M2M cover many areas and the areas are given below:

1. **Security :** Surveillances, Alarm systems, Access control, Car/driver security
2. **Tracking & Tracing :** Fleet Management, Order Management, Pay as you drive, Asset Tracking, Navigation, Traffic information, Road tolling, Traffic optimization/steering
3. **Payment :** Point of sales, Vending machines, Gaming machines
4. **Health :** Monitoring vital signs, Supporting the aged or handicapped, Web Access Telemedicine points, Remote diagnostics
5. **Remote Maintenance/Control :** Sensors, Lighting, Pumps, Valves, Elevator control, Vending machine control, Vehicle diagnostics
6. **Metering :** Power, Gas, Water, Heating, Grid control, Industrial metering
7. **Manufacturing :** Production chain monitoring and automation
8. **Facility Management :** Home/building/campus automation

Difference between IoT and M2M

Sl.No.	IoT	M2M
1	Network of physical devices, vehicles, home appliances, and other items embedded with electronics, software, sensors, actuators, and connectivity.	Direct communication between devices using any communications channel including wired and wireless.
2	Point to point.	Cloud(HTTP).
3	IoT is more about things for example sensors and other cyber-based physical systems.	M2M is all about machines for example smartphones, and appliances
4	IoT is more software based.	M2M is more hardware based.
5	Devices require an active Internet connection.	Devices do not necessarily rely on Internet connection.
6	Unlimited Integration Options.	Limited Integration Options.
7	Semi-Structured and unstructured data.	Structured data.
8	Complex applications and data analysis	Connected devices and associated application

Issues/Concerns in M2M

The key concerns in M2M are addressing and security. The M2M System supports more than one naming scheme. It should also support identification of connected devices or groups of connected devices by their *names, temporary id, pseudonym* (*i.e.* different names for the same entity), *location or combination thereof* (*e.g.* URIs or IMSI). It shall be possible to reuse names for certain classes of devices or for devices operating in certain (*i.e.*resource constrained) environments. The addressing schemes should include:

- IP address of connected objects
- IP address of group of connected objects (including multicast address)
- E.164 addresses of connected objects (*e.g.* MSISDN)

It is expected that M2M devices would typically operate unmanned and unguarded by humans and thus are subject to increased levels of security threats, such as *physical tampering, hacking, unauthorized monitoring, etc.* Terminal devices may also get geographically dispersed over time. Such M2M devices should therefore provide adequate security to detect and resist attacks. Devices may also need to support remote management including firmware updates to correct faults or recover from malicious attacks. Some M2M Equipments (M2Mes) are typically required to be *small, inexpensive, able to operate unattended by humans for extended periods of time, and to communicate over the wireless area network (WAN) or WLAN.* M2Mes are typically deployed in the field for many years, and after deployment, tend to require remote management of their functionality. It is likely that M2Mes will be deployed in very large quantities, and many of them will also be mobile, making it unrealistic or impossible for operators or subscribers to send personnel to manage or service them. These requirements introduce a number of unique security vulnerabilities for the M2Mes and the wireless communication networks over which they communicate.

2

Components

IoT DEVICE

IoT is an ecosystem of physical objects (Things) that are connected and accessible through the Internet. IoT devices are computing/non-computing devices in the Internet of things that have unique identities to connect to a network. It can exchange data with other connected devices and applications. The scope of the IoT is extended to connect different physical things (Anything and Everything). The 'things' in IoT could be objects that have been assigned an IP address and have the ability to collect and transfer data over a network without manual assistance or intervention. The low power embedded technology in the devices helps them to communicate and sense their internal state or the external environment.

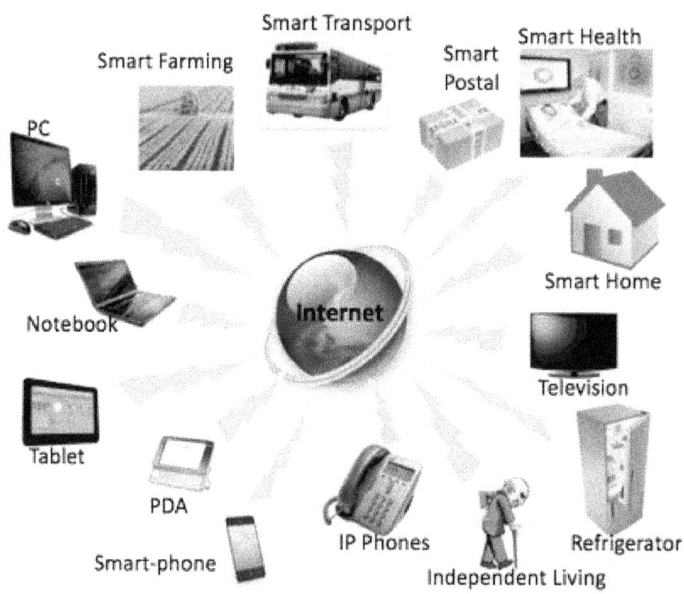

EXAMPLES OF IoT DEVICES

Building Blocks of an IoT Device

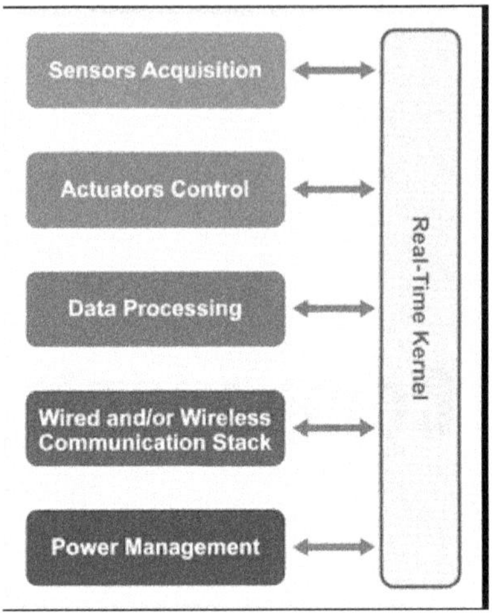

An IoT device consists of a number of modules based on functional attributes, such as:

Sensing

Sensors sense the different parameters of the physical environment. A sensor detects the changes in the ambient conditions or in the state of another device or a system and forwards or processes this information in a certain matter. Sensors are fabricated. Sensor performs some input functions by sensing or feeling the physical changes in a characteristic of a system in response to stimuli. Sensors can be either on-board the IoT device or attached to the device. The sensed information can be communicated either to other devices or cloud-based servers/storage. A sensor converts physical energy like heat, sound, pressure, *etc.*, into electrical energy. An electronic circuit connects to the input at a sensor. The output is according to the variation in physical condition. A smart sensor includes the electronic circuit within itself and includes computing and communication capabilities.

Examples of Sensor

- Temperature
- Humidity
- Distance
- Light
- Acceleration
- Vibrations and Shocks
- Angular Acceleration and change in sensor
- Orientation and Direct compass
- Magnetic sensors/Magnetometer

- ✯ Electric current
- ✯ Sound

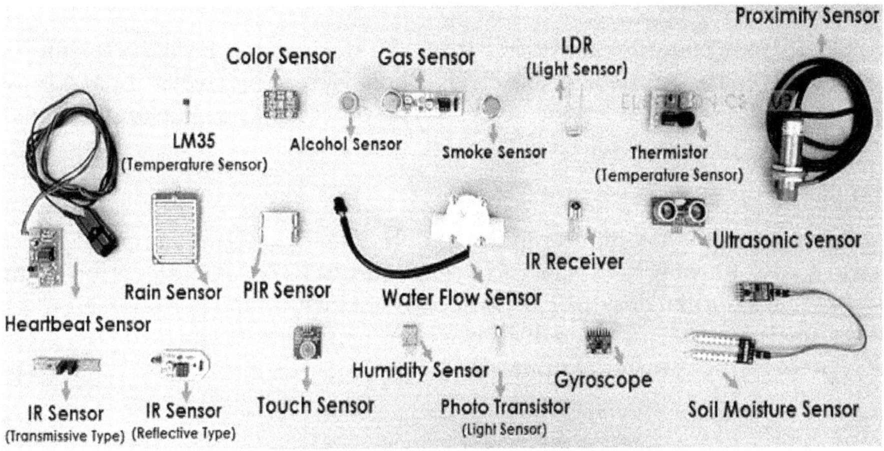

Types of Sensors

Actuation

Based on reading of sensor some action might be needed to be taken which is done by actuators. Actuator is a component of machine or system that moves or controls the mechanism or the system. Actuators need control signals or source of energy.

After receiving control signal:

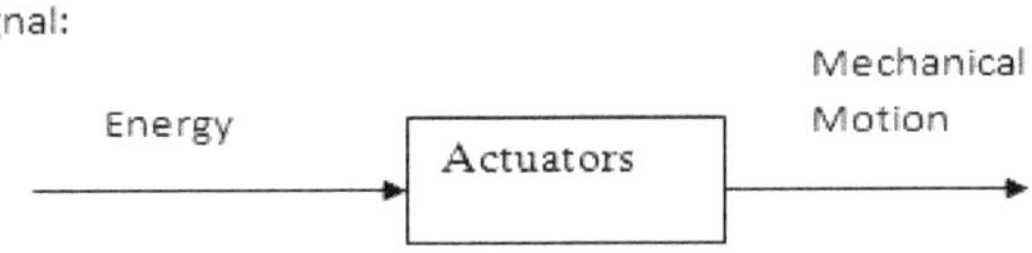

The control system can be simple, software based or human. IoT devices can have various types of actuators attached that allow taking actions upon the physical entities in the vicinity of the device. Actuators can be categorised by the energy source they require to generate motion. For example:

- ✯ Pneumatic actuators use compressed air to generate motion
- ✯ Hydraulic actuators use liquid to generate motion
- ✯ Electric actuators use an external power source, such as battery to generate motion
- ✯ Thermal actuators use a heat source to generate motion

Communication

Comunication modules are responsible for sending collected data to other devices or cloud-based servers/storage and receiving data from other devices and commands from remote applications. Things communicate with one another through wireless technology like WIFI.

Analysis & Processing

Organised data after acquiring from the devices can be used for multiple purposes. Applications usually use the data of devices in two ways- for monitoring, reporting and rule-based actions. Analysis and processing modules are responsible for making sense of the collected data.

RASPBERRY Pi

Raspberry Pi is a computer in the arm. It is a single board computer which is easy to access. Raspberry Pi runs various flavours of Linux and can perform almost all tasks that a normal desktop can do. It does not include any peripherals but some accessories have been included. It allows interfacing sensors and actuators through the general purpose Input/Output pins.

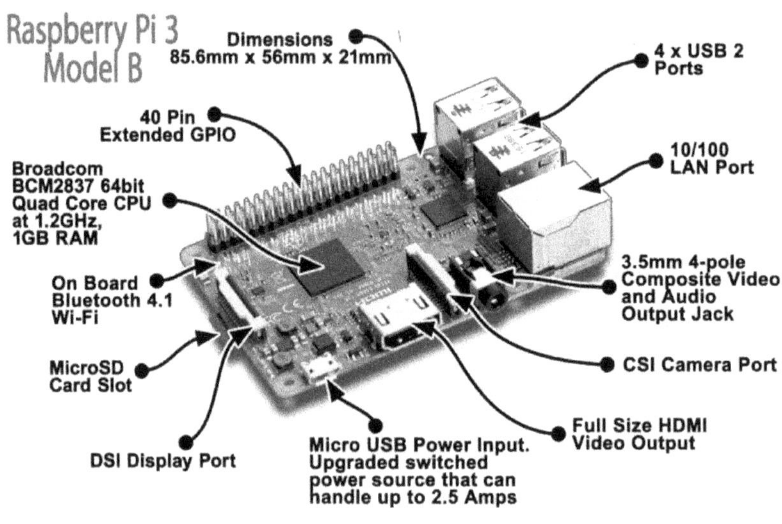

Components of Raspberry Pi

The various components of Raspberry pi are:

- GPIO Pins
- Processor & RAM
- RCA
- Audio out
- Status LEDs
- USB
- HDMI
- Power

- ★ SD cardslot
- ★ Ethernet

GPIO Pins

A powerful feature of the Raspberry Pi is the row of GPIO (general-purpose input/output) pins along the top edge of the board. A 40-pin GPIO header is found on all current Raspberry Pi boards (unpopulated on Pi Zero and Pi Zero W). Prior to the Pi 1 Model B+ (2014), boards comprised a shorter 26-pin header. GPIO Pins act as both digital input and digital output. Raspberry Pi comes with a number of general purpose input/output pins.

Voltages

Two 5V pins and two 3V3 pins are present on the board, as well as a number of ground pins (0V), which are not configurable. The remaining pins are all general purpose 3V3 pins, meaning outputs are set to 3V3 and inputs are 3V3 tolerant.

Inputs

A GPIO pin designated as an input pin can be read as high (3V3) or low (0V). This is made easier with the use of internal pull-up or pull-down resistors. Pins GPIO2 and GPIO3 have fixed pull-up resistors, but for other pins this can be configured in software.

Outputs

A GPIO pin designated as an output pin can be set to high (3V3) or low (0V)

There are four types of pins on Raspberry Pi. As well as simple input and output devices, the GPIO pins can be used with a variety of alternative functions, some are available on all pins, others on specific pins

- ★ True GPIO pins
- ★ I2C interface pins
- ★ SPI interface pins
- ★ Serial Rx and Tx pins

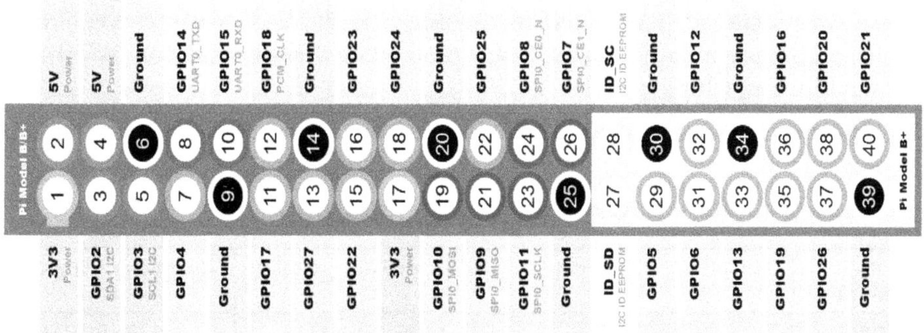

Raspberry Pi-PIN CONFIGURATION

Processor & RAM

The Central processing unit is the **brain of the raspberry pi board** and that is responsible for carrying out the instructions of the computer through logical and mathematical operations. This is a Broadcom BCM2835 System on a Chip (SoC) that is made up of an ARM central processing unit (CPU) and a Videocore 4 graphics processing unit (GPU). The CPU handles all the computations that make a computer work (taking input, doing calculations and producing output), and the GPU handles graphics output.

RCA: An RCA jack allows connection of analog TVs and other similar output devices.

Audio out: This is a standard 3.55-millimeter jack for connection of audio output devices such as headphones or speakers. There is no audio in.

Status LEDs: Raspberry Pi has five status LEDs

Status LED	Functions
PWR	3.3V Power is present
ACT	SD card access
FDX	Full Duplex LAN Connected
100	100 Mbit LAN connected
LNK	Link/Network connected

USB: This is a common connection port for peripheral devices of all types including your mouse and keyboard. Model A has one, and Model B has two. A USB hub can be used to expand the number of ports or plug your mouse into your keyboard if it has its own USB port. Many of the features that are missing, such as WiFi and audio in, can be added using the USB port(s) or a USB hub as needed.

HDMI: This connector allows to hook up a high-definition television or other compatible device using an HDMI cable.

Power: This is a 5v Micro USB power connector into which the compatible power supply can be pluged.

SD cardslot: This is a full-sized SD card slot. An SD card with an operating system (OS) installed is required for booting the device. They are available for purchase from the manufacturers, but an OS can be downloaded and saved to the card if a Linux machine is there.

Ethernet: This connector allows for wired network access and is only available on the Model B.

Comparison among various models of Raspberry Pi:

Key Features	Raspberry Pi3 model B	Raspberry Pi2 model B	Raspberry Pi3 model B
RAM	1GB SDRAM	1GB SDRAM	512 MB SDRAM
CPU	Quadcortex *A53@1.2GHz*	Quadcortex A53@900MHz	ARM11@1GHz

Key Features	Raspberry Pi3 model B	Raspberry Pi2 model B	Raspberry Pi3 model B
GPU	400MHz video core IV	250MHz video core IV	250MHz video core IV
Ethernet	10/100	10/100	None
Wireless	802.11/Bluetooth4.0	None	None
Video output	HDMI/Composite	HDMI/Composite	HDMI/Composite
GPIO	40	40	40

Basic Architecture:

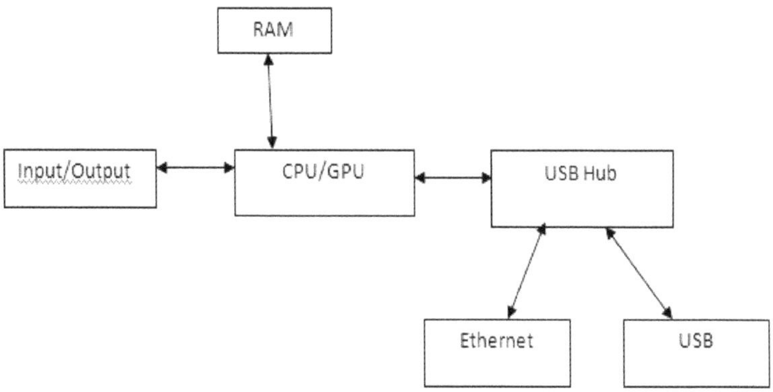

Raspberry Pi-Architecture

RASPBERRY Pi INTERFACES

Raspberry Pi has the following interfaces for the data transfer

- Serial
- SPI (Serial Peripheral Interface)
- I2C

Serial Interface

The serial interface on Raspberry Pi has receive (Rx) and transmit (Tx) pins for communication with serial peripherals. The two pins are made available on GPIO header. To connect to another serial device the 'transmit' of one to the 'receive' of the other and vice-versa.

Serial Peripheral Interface

The Serial Peripheral Interface (SPI) is a communication protocol used to transfer data between micro-computers like the Raspberry Pi and peripheral devices. These peripheral devices may be either sensors or actuators.

SPI uses 4 separate connections to communicate with the target device. These connections are the

- Serial clock (CLK)

- Master Input Slave Output (MISO)
- Master Output Slave Input (MOSI) and
- Chip Select (CS).
- The **clock pin** sense pulses at a regular frequency, the speed at which the Raspberry Pi and SPI device agree to transfer data to each other. For the ADC, clock pulses are sampled on their rising edge, on the transition from low to high.
- The **MISO pin** is a data pin used for the master (in this case the Raspberry Pi) to receive data from the ADC. Data is read from the bus after every clock pulse.
- The **MOSI pin** sends data from the Raspberry Pi to the ADC. The ADC will take the value of the bus on the rising edge of the clock. This means the value must be set before the clock is pulsed.
- Finally, the **Chip Select** line chooses which particular SPI device is in use. If there are multiple SPI devices, they can all share the same CLK, MOSI, and MISO. However, only the selected device has the Chip Select line set low, while all other devices have their CS lines set high. A high Chip Select line tells the SPI device to ignore all of the commands and traffic on the rest of the bus.

I2C

Inter-integrated Circuit protocol is a hardware protocol designed to allow multiple, slave integrated circuits to communicate with one or more master. It is a useful bus that allows data exchange between microcontrollers and peripherals with a minimum of wiring. It uses the following two bidirectional open-drain lines, pulled up with resistors

- Serial Data Line (SDA)
- Serial Clock Line (SCL)

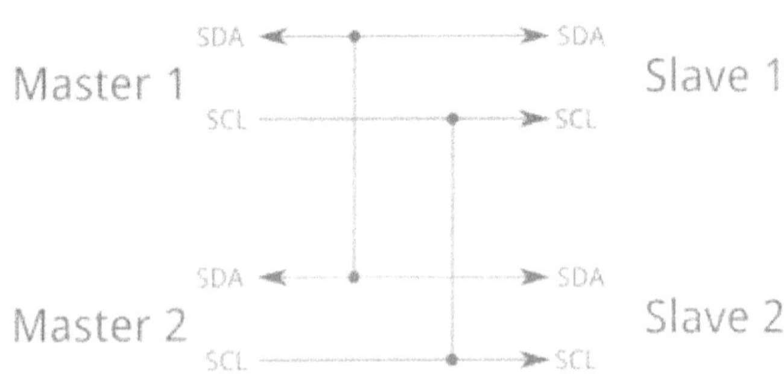

Serial Data and Clock Line

Comparison between SPI and I2C

SPI	I2C
Needs 4 pins for the communication, and additional slave select logic for selecting slaves	Requires only 2 pins to connect any number of slaves
Good for high data rate **full-duplex** (simultaneous sending and receiving of data) connections, supporting clock rates upwards of 10MHz (and thus, 10 million bits per second) for some devices, and the speed scales nicely	I2C supports multi-master hardware connection which is useful for industrial applications where one sensor needs to be controlled and accessed by multiple master devices

LINUX ON RASPBERRY Pi

Raspberry Pi supports various flavours of Linux. The official supported OS are

- Raspbian
- NOOBS

Raspbian

Raspbian is a free operating system based on Debian optimized for the Raspberry Pi hardware. There are several versions of Raspbian including Raspbian Stretch and Raspbian Jessie.

RASPBIAN

Raspberry Pi setup

Download:

https://www.raspberrypi.org/downloads/

Unzip the file and end up with an .img file

Raspberry Pi OS setup

Write Raspbian in SD card:

- Install "Win 32 Disk Imager" software in Windows machine
- Run win32 Disk Imager
- Plug SD card into PC
- Select the device
- Browse the Image File (Raspbian image)

- Write the disc image to the SD card

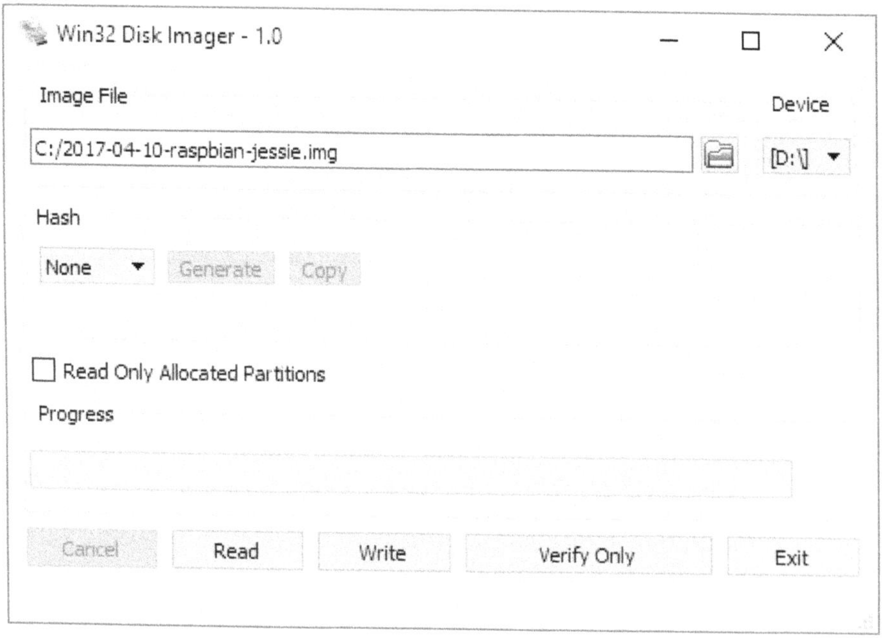

Basic Initial Configuration

Enable SSH

- Open command prompt and type sudo raspberry pi config and expand the file system because the images are compressed
- Goto interface option and select SSH
- Windows based system: Putty or any SSH plant from Ubuntu based system

NOOBS

NOOBS is an easy operating system installer which contains Raspbian and LibreELEC. It also provides a selection of alternative operating systems which are then downloaded from the Internet and installed.

NOOBS Lite contains the same operating system installer without Raspbian pre-loaded. It provides the same operating system selection menu allowing Raspbian and other images to be downloaded and installed.

NOOBS

Third Party OS

Some of the third party OS are

UBUNTU Mate

Ubuntu MATE is a free and open-source Linux distribution. It is an official derivative of Ubuntu. The difference between Ubuntu mate and Ubuntu is that it uses the MATE(a desktop environment composed of free and open-source software that runs on Linux and most BSD derivatives) as its default user interface, based on GNOME 2

UBUNTU MATE

Snappy Ubuntu Core

Ubuntu Core is a version of Ubuntu designed for IOT and embedded devices and uses the Snap store to install software. Ubuntu Core is an ideal OS to use on a Raspberry Pi 3 due to its extremely small size and light weight, plus the added benefit of having Snappy installed and ready after install

SNAPPY UBUNTU CORE

Windows10 core

Windows IoT Core is a version of Windows 10 that is optimized for smaller devices with or without a display that runs on both ARM and x86/x64 devices. Windows 10 IoT offers two editions - **Windows 10 IoT Core** and **Windows 10 IoT Enterprise** - that allow the flexibility in choosing the right specifications for the devices

WINDOWS 10 IOT CORE

PiNet

PiNet is a system that is used to setup and manage Raspberry Pi networks, to replicate similar systems already in place for Windows networks. PiNet is completely free and open source. It can be used for what you want, where you want for no cost and have access to the full source code

PINET

RISC OS

RISC OS is an operating system which was designed specifically for the ARM processor. It is fast, compact and efficient. RISC OS is not a version of Linux, nor is it in any way related to Windows. It has a number of unique features and aspects to its design.

RISC OS

Applications of Raspberry Pi

The raspberry pi boards are used in many applications like Media streamer, Arcade machine, Tablet computer, Home automation, Internet radio,

Controlling robots, Cosmic Computer, Hunting for meteorites, Coffee and also in raspberry pi based projects. Few other applications are

- Media Streamer
- Home Automation
- Desktop
- Wireless Print Server
- Gaming machine
- Robot controller
- FM radio station

Advantages

- Although Raspberry Pi is as small as the size of a credit card, it works as if a normal computer at a relatively low price.
- It is possible to work as a low-cost server to handle light internal or web traffic.
- Grouping a set of Raspberry Pi to work as a server is more cost-effective than a normal server.
- If all light traffic servers are changed into Raspberry Pi, it can certainly minimize an enterprise's budget.

Disadvantages

Even though Raspberry Pi can perform different tasks, there are some limitations due to its hardware.

- Because of its processor, it cannot run X86 operating systems.
- Some common ones like Windows and Linux distros are not compatible.
- Some applications which require high demands on CPU processing are off-limits.
- It can work as a personal computer, but cannot replace it.

Comparison between Raspberry Pi and Aurdino

Raspberry Pi

- is more powerful in terms of computation or processing power
- has better memory capacity
- can integrate different types of sensors and actuators
- cost is more than Aurdino
- Consumes more power

PROGRAMMING RASPBERRY Pi WITH PYTHON

Python

Python is one of the most popular programming language and useful language. Python is very easy to use *i.e.* it has an easy to read syntax and writing programs. Python is simple for programmers as they need to write few lines of code when compared to other popular programming languages like C, C++ or Java

Python is one of the highly recommended programming languages for people who are new to coding as its syntax is very clean with its importance to readability and usage of simple English keywords.

The frequently used commands on Raspberry Pi

Commands	Functions
ls	The ls command lists the content of the current directory (or one that is specified). It can be used with the -l - To display additional information (permissions, owner, group, size, date and timestamp of last edit) about each file and directory in a list format -a - To view files beginning with . (*i.e.* dotfiles).
Cd	Changes the current directory to the one specified. It can be Relative (*i.e.* cd directoryA) Absolute (*i.e.* cd/home/pi/directoryA) paths
Pwd	The pwd command displays the name of the present working directory on a Raspberry Pi Example: pwd will output something like/home/pi
Mkdir	It is used to create a new directory Example: mkdir raj would create the directory raj in the present working directory
Rmdir	To remove directories, use rmdir. Example: rmdir psn will remove the directory psn only if it is empty.
Rm	The command rm removes the specified file (or recursively from a directory when used with -r)
Cp	Using cp makes a copy of a file and places it at the specified location). Example: cp ~/adhi/home/otherUser/would copy the file adhi from the home directory to that of the user otherUser (assuming you have permission to copy it there).
Mv	The mv command moves a file and places it at the specified location (so where cp performs a 'copy-paste', mv performs a 'cut-paste'). The usage is similar to cp. Example: mv ~/Adhi/home/otherUser/would move the file Adhi from the home directory to that of the user otherUser. This command is also useful as a method to rename files and directories after they've been created
Touch	The command touch sets the last modified time-stamp of the specified file(s) or creates it if it does not already exist.
Cat	Cat can be used to list the contents of file(s), *e.g.* cat thisFile will display the contents of thisFile. Can be used to list the contents of multiple files, *i.e.* cat *.txt will list the contents of all .txt files in the current directory
Head	The head command displays the beginning of a file. Can be used with -n to specify the number of lines to show (by default ten), or with -c to specify the number of bytes.
Tail	The opposite of head, tail displays the end of a file. The starting point in the file can be specified either through -b for 512 byte blocks, -c for bytes, or -n for number of lines

Chmod	chmod can be used to change the permissions for a file. The chmod command can use symbols u (user that owns the file), g (the files group) , and o (other users) and the permissions r (read), w (write), and x (execute). Using chmod u+x *filename* will add execute permission for the owner of the file
Chown	The chown command changes the user and/or group that owns a file. It normally needs to be run as root using sudo *e.g.* sudo chown pi:root *filename* will change the owner to pi and the group to root.
Ssh	ssh denotes the secure shell. Connect to another computer using an encrypted network connection.
Scp	The scp command copies a file from one computer to another using ssh.
Sudo	The sudo command enables you to run a command as a superuser, or another user. Use sudo -s for a superuser shell.
Dd	The dd command copies a file converting the file as specified. It is often used to copy an entire disk to a single file or back again. So, for example, dd if=/dev/sdd of=backup. img will create a backup image from an SD card or USB disk drive at/dev/sdd.
Df	Use df to display the disk space available and used on the mounted filesystems. Use df -h to see the output in a human-readable format using M for MBs rather than showing number of bytes.
Unzip	The unzip command extracts the files from a compressed zip file.
Tar	Use tar to store or extract files from a tape archive file. It can also reduce the space required by compressing the file similar to a zip file.
Pipes	A pipe allows the output from one command to be used as the input for another command. The pipe symbol is a vertical line |. For example, to only show the first ten entries of the ls command it can be piped through the head command ls | head
Tree	Use the tree command to show a directory and all subdirectories and files indented as a tree structure.
&	Run a command in the background with &, freeing up the shell for future commands.
Wget	Download a file from the web directly to the computer with wget. So wget https://www. raspberrypi.org/documentation/linux/usage/commands.md will download this file to your computer as commands.md
Curl	Use curl to download or upload a file to/from a server. By default, it will output the file contents of the file to the screen.
Man	Show the manual page for a file with man. To find out more, run man man to view the manual page of the man command.
Grep	Use grep to search inside files for certain search patterns. For example, grep "search" *.txt will look in all the files in the current directory ending with .txt for the string search.
Awk	awk is a programming language useful for searching and manipulating text files
Find	The find command searches a directory and subdirectories for files matching certain patterns.
Whereis	Use whereis to find the location of a command. It looks through standard program locations until it finds the requested command
Ping	The ping utility is usually used to check if communication can be made with another host. It can be used with default settings by just specifying a hostname (*e.g.* ping raspberrypi. org) or an IP address (*e.g.* ping 8.8.8.8). It can specify the number of packets to send with the -c flag
Nmap	nmap is a network exploration and scanning tool. It can return port and OS information about a host or a range of hosts. Running just nmap will display the options available as well as example usage.

Hostname	The hostname command displays the current hostname of the system. A privileged (super) user can set the hostname to a new one by supplying it as an argument (*e.g.* hostname new-host)
Ifconfig	Use ifconfig to display the network configuration details for the interfaces on the current system when run without any arguments (*i.e.* ifconfig).

Applications of Raspberry Pi and Python

Some of the popular applications are mentioned below:

- ✯ Learn programming with Python
- ✯ Raspberry Pi as a web server
- ✯ Raspberry Pi Cluster(Super Computer)
- ✯ Application like weather monitoring stations, Home automation by interfacing different sensors
- ✯ Raspberry pi as monitoring and tracking server

Controlling LED with Raspberry Pi

Components Required:

- ✯ One led
- ✯ 300 ohm resistor
- ✯ Jumper cables
- ✯ Bread Board

The Bread Board

The breadboard is a way of connecting electronic components to each other without having to solder them together. They are often used to test a circuit design before creating a Printed Circuit Board (PCB).

The holes on the breadboard are connected in a pattern.

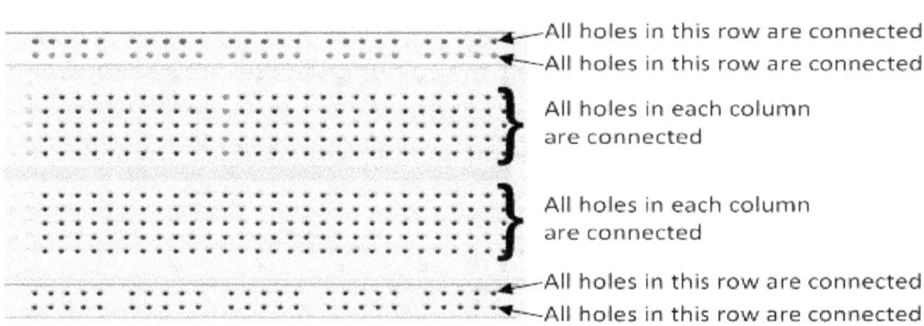

With the breadboard, the top row of holes is all connected together – marked with red dots. And so are the second rows of holes – marked with blue dots. The same goes for the two rows of holes at the bottom of the breadboard.

In the middle, the columns of wires are connected together with a break in the middle. So, for example, all the green holes marked are connected together, but they are not connected to the yellow holes, nor the purple ones. Therefore, any wire you poke into the green holes will be connected to other wires poked into the other green holes.

The LED

LED stands for Light Emitting Diode, and glows when electricity is passed through it. In LED one leg is longer than the other. The longer leg (known as the 'anode'), is always connected to the positive supply of the circuit. The shorter leg (known as the 'cathode') is connected to the negative side of the power supply, known as 'ground'.

LEDs will only work if power is supplied the correct way round (*i.e.* if the 'polarity' is correct). If it did not light in the circuit, it may be because they have been connected the wrong way round

The Resistors

Use resistors to connect LEDs up to the GPIO pins of the Raspberry Pi. The Raspberry Pi can only supply a small current (about 60mA). The LEDs will want to draw more, and if allowed to they will burn out the Raspberry Pi. Therefore putting the resistors in the circuit will ensure that only this small current will flow and the Pi will not be damaged.

Resistors are a way of limiting the amount of electricity going through a circuit; specifically, they limit the amount of 'current' that is allowed to flow. The measure of resistance is called the **Ohm (Ω)**, and the larger the resistance, the more it limits the current. The value of a resistor is marked with coloured bands along the length of the resistor body.

Use a 330Ω resistor. Identify the 330Ω resistors by the colour bands along the body. The colour coding will depend on how many bands are on the resistors supplied:

- If there are four colour bands, they will be Orange, Orange, Brown, and then Gold.
- If there are five bands, then the colours will be Orange, Orange, Black, Black, Brown.

It does not matter which way the resistors are connected. Current flows in both ways through them.

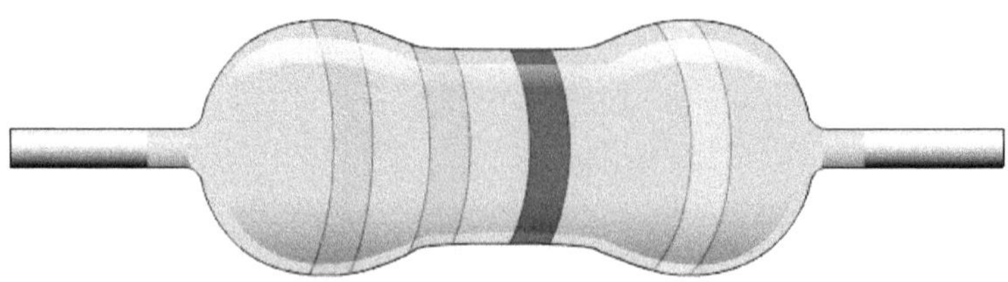

Jumper Wires

Jumper wires are used on breadboards to 'jump' from one connection to another. The jumpers in the circuit have different connectors on each end. The end with the 'pin' will go into the Breadboard. The end with the piece of plastic with a hole in it will go onto the Raspberry Pi's GPIO pins

Building the Circuit

The circuit consists of a power supply (the Pi), an LED that lights when the power is applied, and a resistor to limit the current that can flow through the circuit.

Use one of the 'ground' (GND) pins to act like the 'negative' or 0 volt ends of a battery. The 'positive' end of the battery will be provided by a GPIO pin. Here we will be using pin 18. When they are 'taken high', which means it outputs 3.3 volts, the LED will light

Circuit Diagram

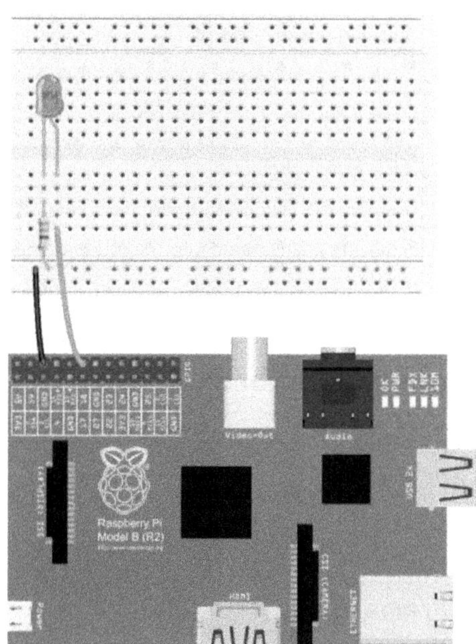

Program

```
import RPi.GPIO as GPIO
import time
GPIO.setmode(GPIO.BCM)
GPIO.setwarnings(False)
GPIO.setup(18,GPIO.OUT)
print "LED on"
GPIO.output(18,GPIO.HIGH)
time.sleep(1)
print "LED off"
GPIO.output(18,GPIO.LOW)
```

Explanation

import RPi.GPIO as GPIO	The first line tells the Python interpreter (the thing that runs the Python code) that it will be using a 'library' that will tell it how to work with the Raspberry Pi's GPIO pins. A 'library' gives a programming language extra commands that can be used to do something different that it previously did not know how to do. This is like adding a new channel to TV so you can watch something different.
import time	Imports the Time library so that the script can be paused later on.
GPIO.setmode(GPIO.BCM)	Each pin on the Pi has several different names, so have to tell the program which naming convention is to be used.
GPIO.setwarnings(False)	This tells Python not to print GPIO warning messages to the screen.
GPIO.setup(18,GPIO.OUT)	This line tells the Python interpreter that pin 18 is going to be used for outputting information, which means you are going to be able to turn the pin 'on' and 'off'.
print "LED on"	This line prints some information to the terminal.
GPIO.output(18,GPIO.HIGH)	This turns the GPIO pin 'on'. What this actually means is that the pin is made to provide power of 3.3volts. This is enough to turn the LED in our circuit on.
time.sleep(1)	Pauses the Python program for 1 second
print "LED off"	This line prints some information to the terminal.
GPIO.output(18,GPIO.LOW)	This turns the GPIO pin 'off', meaning that the pin is no longer supplying any power.

Interfacing PIR Sensor with Raspberry Pi

Program

```
import RPi.GPIO as GPIO
import time
GPIO.setwarnings(False)
GPIO.setmode(GPIO.BOARD)
```

```
GPIO.setup(11,GPIO.IN)              #Read output from PIR motion sensor
GPIO.setup(3,GPIO.OUT)              #LED output pin
While True:
i=GPIO.input(11)
if i==0:                       #When output from motion sensor is LOW
print "No intruders",i
GPIO.output(3, 0)              #Turn OFF LED
time.sleep(0.1)
elif i==1:                     #When output from motion sensor is HIGH
print "Intruder detected",i
GPIO.output(3, 1)              #Turn ON LED
time.sleep(0.1)
```

Circuit Diagram

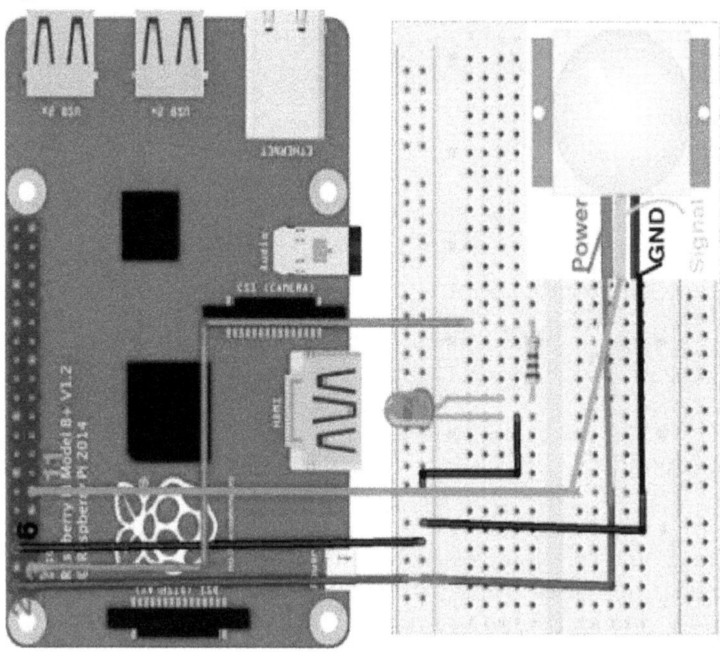

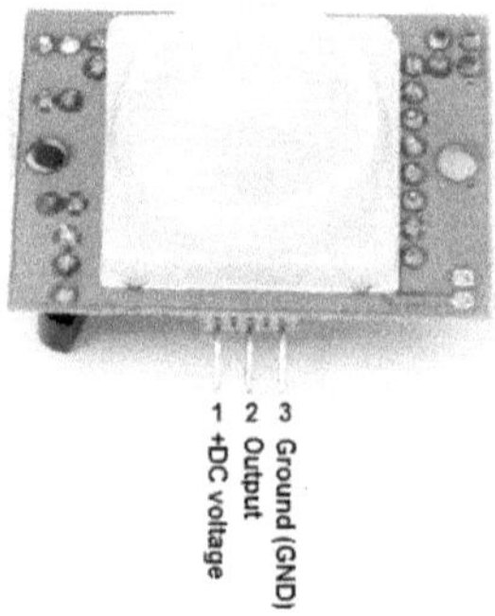

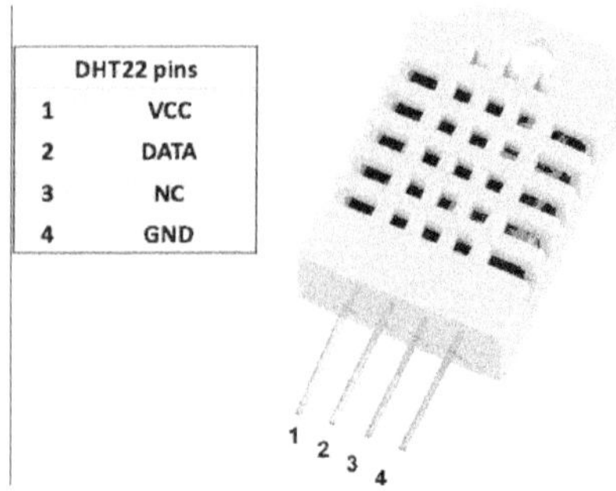

PIR Sensor

Temperature Dependent Auto-Cooling System

Components Required

- ✯ DHT Sensor
- ✯ 4.7K ohm Resistor
- ✯ Relay
- ✯ Jumper wires
- ✯ RaspberryPi
- ✯ Mini Fan

DHT Sensor: Digital Humidity and Temperature Sensor

Pin1, 2, 3, 4 from left to right

PIN 1-3.3V to 5V Power Supply

PIN 2-Data

PIN 3-NULL

PIN 4-Ground

Relay

It is an Electro-mechanical switch. It has got three output terminals. The composite board consists of many different relays. There are actually four relays. Therefore four different devices can be connected to it. This single entity is known as one relay and in electronic this is a sugar cube relay generally called as sugar cube relays ranging from operating voltage as of 6 volts upto 12 volts. There are three terminals corresponding to each relay. So, from left to right

- ✯ The first terminal is designated as Normal Open or no
- ✯ The middle one is Common
- ✯ The third terminal is known as Normally Close

Circuit Connections

- Connect the VCC pin of relay to the 5V supply pin of RaspberryPi
- Connect the ground pin of the relay to the ground pin of RaspberryPi
- Connect the input/signal pin of relay to the assigned output pin of Raspberry Pi

For RaspberryPi an additional library from Adafruit is needed, which basically supplied this sensor. For DHT22 sensor in Raspberry Pi, Adafruit DHT sensor library need to be installed using the following command

Note: Since python base scripting is used, DHT python library must be implemented

Steps to install the library in your Pi

- Get the clone from GIT

  Git clone https://github.com/adafruit/Adafruit_Python_DHT.git

- Go to folder Adafruit_Python_DHT

  Cd Adafruit_Python_DHT

- Install the library

  Sudo python setup.py install

DHT22 with Pi

```
Import RPI.GPIO as GPIO
From time import sleep
Import Adafruit_DHT
GPIO.setmode(GPIO.BOARD)
GPIO.setwarnings(False)
Sensor=Adafruit_DHT.AM2302
Print('Getting data from sensor')
Humidity,temperature=Adafruit_DHT.read_retry(sensor,4)
Print('Temp={0.01f}*C humidity={1:0.1f}%'.format(temperature, humidity))
```

Connection: Relay

Set the GPIO pin connected with the relay's input pin as output in the sketch

GPIO.setup(11,GPIO.OUT)

Set the relay pin high when the temperature is greater than 30

```
if temperature>30
print('Temp>30')
GPIO.output(FAN,0)
Print('Fan On')
Sleep(5)
Print("FAN OFF")
GPIO.output(FAN,1)
Else:
GPIO.output(FAN,1)
Print('Temp below max value.FAN OFF')
```

Connection: Fan

Connect the Li-po battery in series with the fan

- NO terminal of the relay->positive terminal of the fan
- Common terminal of the relay->Positive terminal of the battery
- Negative terminal of the battery->Negative terminal of the fan

Noise and Air pollution Monitoring System

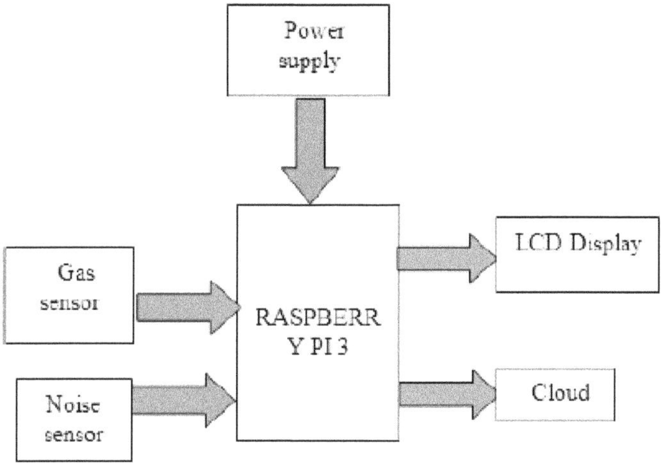

Gas Sensor

Gas Sensor (MQ2) module is useful for gas leakage detection (home and industry). It is suitable for detecting hydrogen (H2), Liquid Petroleum Gas (LPG), methane (CH4), Carbon monoxide (CO), Alcohol, Smoke or Propane. Due to its high sensitivity and fast response time, measurement can be taken as soon as possible. The sensitivity of the sensor can be adjusted by potentiometer

Noise Sensor

The sound sensor module provides an easy way to detect sound and is generally used for detecting sound intensity. This module can be used for security, switch, and monitoring applications. Its accuracy can be easily adjusted for the convenience of usage. When the sensor detects a sound, it processes an output signal voltage which is sent to a raspberry pi then performs necessary processing

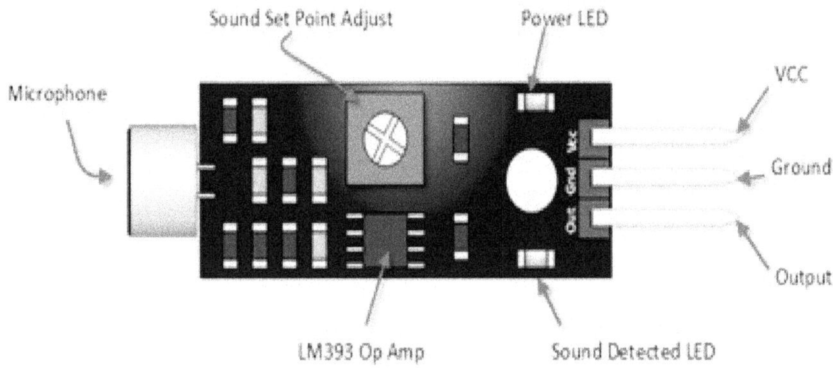

Use raspberry pi 3 as embedded device for sensing and storing the data in cloud. Raspberry pi connects the embedded device to Internet and sensors are connected. The corresponding sensors read to its digital value and from digital value the corresponding environmental parameters will be evaluated. The raspberry pi 3 has inbuilt wifi module to transfer sensor data to the end user.

APIs/PACKAGES

The easiest way to manage installing, upgrading and removing software is using APT (Advanced Packaging Tool) from Debian. If a piece of software is packaged in Debian and it works on the Raspberry Pi's ARM architecture, it should also be available in Raspbian.

To install or remove packages, the root user permission is needed. It must be logged in as sudousers or root.

APT keeps a list of software sources on Pi in a file at/etc/apt/sources.list

- ★ Before installing software, update the package list using **sudo apt-get update**
- ★ To install a package with APT, **sudo apt-get install tree.** Tree is a command line tool which provides a visualisation of the structure of the current directory
- ★ Typing **man tree gives the manual entry for the package tree**
- ★ Typing **whereis tree** shows where tree lives:
- ★ Uninstalling a package with APT, give REMOVE(**sudo apt-get remove tree**)
- ★ To remove the package and its associated configuration files, **sudo apt-get purge tree**
- ★ If software updates are available, **sudo apt-get update** is used
- ★ To upgrade specific package, without upgrading all the other out-of-date package at the same time, give **sudo apt-get install** somepackage
- ★ **apt-cache search** package name to search the archives for a package with a given keyword
- ★ **apt-cache show:** to view more information about a package

Note:

- ✯ Use appropriately sized SD card.
- ✯ A lock should be performed while software is installing, so multiple packages cant be installed at the same time

Web Services

Designing a RESTful Web API

One of the most useful reasons for providing the Raspberry Pi with a REST API is to expose its inputs and outputs to a web client (on any iPhone, laptop or desktop PC anywhere in the world) for remote monitoring and/or control.

REST

Now-a-days, the Web has turned from a network of web servers serving mainly static pages to web browsers into a full client-server architecture, where single-page client web apps use AJAX principles to communicate with server-side applications, increasingly via simple but powerful RESTful APIs.

REST On RaspberryPi

Node.JS is used in the backend (server-side) framework for building single-page or client-server web apps and more recently as a Javascript platform on Raspberry Pi. On top of providing the advantage of an asynchronous, event-based programming model, Javascript is used in the frontend and the backend and on the Pi.

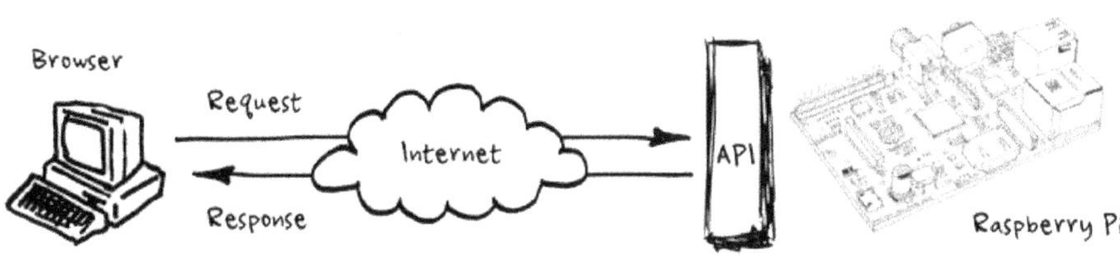

Installation of Node.JS on Raspbery Pi

Installing node on the RPi is not difficult and no longer requires patches to the standard source or even a local compile.The Raspberry Pi's CPU is based on ARMv6

1. Start by getting the URL to the pre-built binaries that need to be be installed. The latest version can be found at http://nodejs.org/download/
2. Node needs to be installed using the command line interface on Raspberry Pi

3. Download the Node tar file identified above using wget, then go to the/user/local directory and unpack the tar file there, as shown in the following steps:

   $wget http://nodejs.org/dist/v0.8.21/node-v0.8.21-linux-arm-pi.tar.gz

   $cd/usr/local

   $sudo tar xzvf ~/node-v0.8.21-linux-arm-pi.tar.gz --strip=1

   Verify the installation of Node.JS by typing:

   $ node –v => displays the Node version number

   $ npm –v =>should show the version of the Node Package Manager

Coding a RESTful API example on the Raspberry Pi

Example: Client-Server application using Raspberry Pi as the server.

To build the REST example, create three source files on Raspberry Pi:

* The server-side Javascript code (server.js)
* HTML page (index.html)
* client-side Javascript (client.js)

server.js – Server-side Javascript code uses the Node and the Express framework to provide simplistic Web server functionality and to expose a RESTful API.

index.html – The HTML page which the browser loads from the Raspberry Pi and uses to render the presentation layer for the application.

client.js – Javascript code executed in the browser when our HTML page loads. This code implements the AJAX client functionality to call API and render the results directly in the HTML page.

The application architecture looks like this:

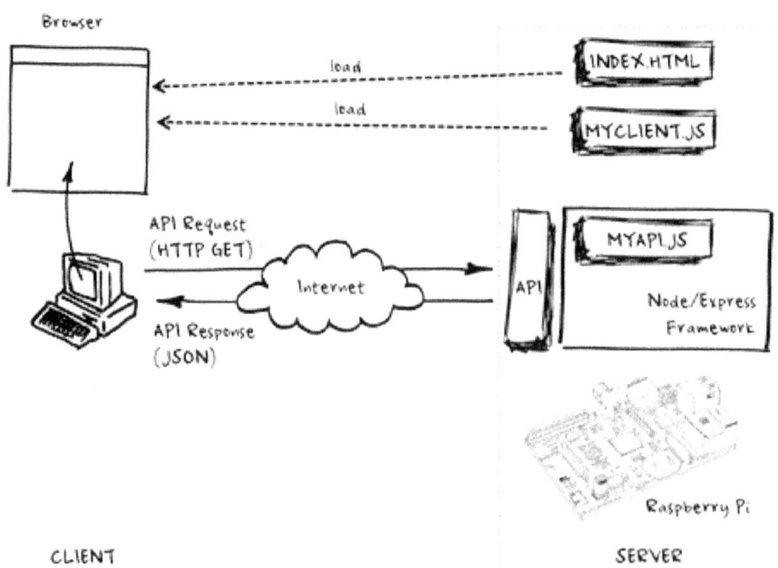

The Server (RPi) -side code

Create a file called *server.js* on Pi and copy the code below to build a simple server in Javascript, which processes API requests on port 3000 with a JSON object. (Port 3000 is the standard port most commonly used for an express server).

Use *http* and *express* packages to let Node know, call express to create the application server as an object, and assign it to a variable.

```
var http = require('http');
var express = require('express');
var app = express();
```

Define an array of objects the client will be able to query....

```
var inputs = [{ pin: '11', gpio: '17', value: 1 },
        { pin: '12', gpio: '18', value: 0 }];
```

Then configure Express to serve index.html and any other static pages stored in the home directory, such as client.js JavaScript source file

```
 app.use(express['static'](__dirname ));
```

Next define the API middleware for server-side application. Use express's get function to define routes for the API calls and/or page requests to our server.

```
//Express route for incoming requests for a customer name
app.get('/inputs/:id', function(req, res) {
 res.status(200).send(inputs[req.params.id]);
});
//Express route for any other unrecognised incoming requests
app.get('*', function(req, res) {
 res.status(404).send('Unrecognised API call');
});
//Express route to handle errors
app.use(function(err, req, res, next) {
 if (req.xhr) {
  res.status(500).send('Oops, Something went wrong!');
 } else {
  next(err);
 }
});
```

Finally, start the server application, listening on port 3000:

```
app.listen(3000);
console.log('App Server running at port 3000');
```

INDEX.HTML: the homepage

The web page simply displays a title, and sets up an input div as a placeholder that will be used by the client-side JavaScript code in client.js to display the I/O values retrieved from RPi.

```
<!DOCTYPE html>
<html lang="en">
 <head>
  <meta charset="utf-8"/>
  <title>My Express API server example</title>
  <script src="http://code.jquery.com/jquery-latest.js"></script>
  <script src="client.js"></script>
 </head>
 <body>
  <H1>My Express API server example</H1>
  <div id="input"></div>
 </body>
</html>
```

CLIENT.JS: the client-side code

The JavaScript code will be loaded and executed on the client machine when the browser loads our HTML page. It makes call to API server running on the Raspberry Pi to retrieve and display the state of two inputs.

```
window.onload = function () {
 var url,
   i,
   jqxhr;
 for (i = 0; i < 2; i++) {
  url = document.URL + 'inputs/' + i;
  jqxhr = $.getJSON(url, function(data) {
   console.log('API response received');
   $('#input').append('<p>input gpio port ' + data['gpio'] + ' on pin ' +
    data['pin'] + ' has current value ' + data['value'] + '</p>');
  });
 }
};
```

Running Raspberry Pi Web App Server

To start web server on RPi , invoke application with node, from the folder where the source files are saved

$ node myapi.js

App Server running at port 3000

$

Make sure that express module using npm is installed.

Web server will now run continuously in the background, waiting for API calls.

Finally, using another machine on the same local network, open a web browser and navigate to App Server hosted on the RPi.

If the RPi has the local IP address 192.168.0.23 then enter this in the browser:

http://192.168.0.23:3000

This will cause the browser to load your index.html file from the RPi, which then loads the javascript client code in client.js.

3

Tools Used in IoT

Building a complex application is no easy task, especially a connected IoT solution using hardware. It's a crazy world of options out there right now which can induce analysis paralysis. I've worked through the plethora of services to come up with what I believe are some of the best available today. This list covers a variety of different components involved in building a solution.

Tessel 2

Starting at the top of list is a hardware provider that is great for prototyping and building basic solutions. The Tessel 2 is a great way to take advantage of a variety of different sensors and modules. The board supports over a dozen different modules including accelerometer, GPS, RFID, camera and more. One of the best features of the Tessel is that it can programmed using Node.js. This means you can take advantage of your JavaScript skills to create both the hardware firmware and the server solutions.

The Tessel hardware has two processors on it - a 580MHz Mediatek MT7620n and 48MHz Atmel SAMD21 coprocessor. One is running your firmware application at high speed and the enables better I/O control and power management. If you're looking for more of DIY hardware solution, a NodeMCU will be worth a look.

Platformio

The second tool I'd recommend taking a look at will make your life easier when programming the hardware itself. PlatformIO is a cross-platform IoT development environment that includes an IDE, build system, and library manager. The IDE is built on top of the Atom editor or can be installed as a plugin. It has very nice debugging integration and serial port monitor. The platform itself has support for over 200 different boards. The bottom line is that PlatformIO can really speed up your time to delivering your IoT application.

IBM Watson

Next up is a tool you can use to predict the future or understand if people like you in the social world. One of the areas that is going to become increasily important is using predicitive analysis on IoT data. IBM Watson has a set of APIs that help make this simple for developers. The APIs include a host of different services. You can recongize objects in images, understand conversation sentiment, and more. You can check out the entire range here. They've done a great job of continuing to expand useful service for the Internet of Things.

Twilio Programmable Wireless

The fourth tool is a brand new service from one of best developer tool companies out there. Just launched this week at Twilio's Signal Conference is a brand new service for adding cellular connectivity to IoT projects. Twilio Progammable Wireless service includes the ability to provision devices on the fly and control them from anywhere. This is a perfect for a wide range of applications including vehicle tracking and more. The whole thing is pretty cheap as well. SIM cards are $5 to buy and then just $2 per month plus $.10 per MB of data used. If you're looking for something a bit more beefy then they have a larger plan for consuming GBs of data. Note that this service is still in preview mode. This is a space that is heating up as well. There are a number of other options for cellular connectivity including Hologram.

Losant

Losant is an IoT platform for building IoT solutions quickly, easily, and securely. Using the platform you can connect a wide range of abstract hardware, manage tons of devices, store and analyze the data, and take action in real-time. This means you can easily build complex applications on top of the Losant platform.

Dronesmith

Drones are evolving in to one of the most important subjects in the Internet of Things space. They have the potential to change nearly every industry in the world. This next service is aimed at making it so much easier to use drones to solve hard problems. There are several real challenges with utilizing drones to create business solutions. Dronesmith is helping tackle these challenges one by one. Their airbourne computer, Luci, makes it easier to create and customize your own drones.

IFTTT

The last service lets you combine a variety of different applications out there. There are ton of random services out in the world and IFTTT tries to make it easy to make use of them in simple ways. In the smart home world IFTTT has a wide array of support for Wemo, Phillips Hue, Nest, and more. This turns them in to the goto place to easily connect and control those devices. One of my favorite mechanisms for combining IFTTT with other applications is using their webhook support.

4

Open Source Tools for Internet of Things

IoT Development Tools

Arduino

Arduino is an open-source prototyping platform based on easy-to-use hardware and software. It is both a hardware specification for interactive electronics and a set of software that includes an IDE and the Arduino programming language. The website explains that Arduino is "a tool for making computers than can sense and control more of the physical world than your desktop computer."

Eclipse IoT Project

Eclipse is sponsoring several different projects surrounding IoT. They include application frameworks and services; open source implementations of IoT protocols and tools for working with Lua, which Eclipse is promoting as an ideal IoT programming language.

Kinoma

Kinoma, a Marvell Semiconductor hardware prototyping platform encompasses three different open source projects. Kimona Create is a DIY construction kit for prototyping electronic devices. Kimona Studio is the development environment that works with Create and the Kinoma Platform Runtime. Kimona Connect is a free iOS and Android app that links smartphones and tables with IoT devices.

M2MLabs Mainspring

M2MLabs Mainspring is an open source application framework for building machine to machine (M2M) applications such as remote monitoring, fleet management or smart grid.Its capabilities include flexible modeling of devices, device configuration, communication between devices and applications, validation and normalization of data, long-term data storage, and data retrieval functions.

It's based on Java and the Apache Cassandra NoSQL database. M2M applications can be prototyped in hours rather than weeks and finally transfered to a high performance execution environment built on top of a standard J2EE server and the highly scaleable Apache Cassandra database.

Node-RED

A visual tool for wiring the Internet of Things i.e wiring together hardware devices, APIs and online services in new and interesting ways. Built on Node.js, Node-RED describes itself as "a visual tool for wiring the Internet of Things." It allows developers to connect devices, services and APIs together using a browser-based flow editor. It can run on Raspberry Pi, and more than 60,000 modules are available to extend its capabilities.

Hardware

Arduino Yún

Arduino is an open-source electronics platform based on easy-to-use hardware and software. This microcontroller combines the ease of an Arduino-based board with Linux. It includes two processors—the ATmega32u4 (which supports Arduino) and the Atheros AR9331 (which runs Linux). Other features include Wi-Fi, Ethenet support, a USB port, micro-SD card slot, three reset buttons and more.

BeagleBoard

BeagleBoard offers credit-card sized computers that can run Android and Linux. Because they have very low power requirements, they're a good option for IoT devices. Both the hardware designs and the software they run are open source, and BeagleBoard hardware (often sold under the name BeagleBone) is available through a wide variety of distributors. Experiment with Linux, Android and Ubuntu and jump-start development in five minutes with the included USB cable.

Flutter

Flutter is a programmable processor core for electronics projects, designed for hobbysits, students, and engineers.Flutter's claim to fame is its long range. This Arduino-based board has a wireless transmitter that can reach more than a half mile. Plus, you don't need a router; flutter boards can communicate with each other directly. It includes 256-bit AES encryption, and it's easy to use.

LightBlue Bean Punch Through

The LightBlue Bean is a low energy Bluetooth Arduino microcontroller. Using Bluetooth 4.0, it is programmed wirelessly, runs on a coin cell battery, and is perfect for smartphone controlled projects. With Bean, you can program wirelessly from any of your devices. No more unscrewing screws and ungluing glue.

Microduino

Microduino presents the world's smallest series of Arduino-compatible smart modules that are small, flexible, stackable and powerful, and can be used to create a limitless amount of DIY projects. Microduino offers really small boards that are compatible with Arduino.

OpenPicus

OpenPicus is an Italian hardware company who designs and produce Internet of Things system on modules called Flyport. Flyport is open hardware and the openPicus framework and IDE are open software. Its platform and hardware are open source, but its products can be used to create closed source commercial products. The company also offers its development services for hire.

Pinoccio

Arduino-compatible Pinnoccio boards (which the company calls "Scouts") connect to each other in a low-power mesh network. They include a built-in rechargeable battery that can connect to solar panels or any USB power supply. The organization also offers Pinoccio HQ, a GUI for monitoring the activities of the scouts, and ScoutScript, an easy-to-use scripting language for controlling the devices.

RasWIK

Made by a company called Ciseco, RasWIK is short for the Raspberry Pi Wireless Inventors Kit. It allows anyone with a Raspberry Pi to experiment with building their own Wi-Fi-connected devices. It includes documentation for 29 different projects or you can come up with one of your own. There is a fee for the devices, but all of the included code is open source, and you can use it to build commercial products if you choose.

SODAQ

Short for "Solar-Powered Data Acquistion," SADAQ offers Arduino-compatible boards with Lego-like plug-in modules. The website includes a number of tutorials, making it a suitable for beginners. And the solar panel makes it a good choice for logging environmental data in various locations where power and Internet connections might not be available.

Tessel

Tessel aims to make hardware development easier for software developers with this JavaScript-enabled microcontroller that plugs into any USB port. You can also connect it to additional modules to add accelerometer, ambient light and sound, camera, Bluetooth, GPS and/or nine other capabilities.

UDOO

This Arduino-compatible board can also run Android or Linux (a distribution called UDOObuntu) from its second processor. It boasts that it is four times as powerful as a Raspberry Pi. Multiple tutorials and projects are available on the website, and it also offers a "Made by UDOOers" section where people can show off their creations.

Home Automation Software

OpenHAB

OpenHAB lets the smart devices you already have in your home talk to one another. It's vendor- and hardware-neutral, running on any Java-enabled system. One of its goals is to allow users to add new features to their devices and combine them in new ways. It's won several awards, and it has a companion cloud computing service called my.openHAB.

The Thing System

It promises to find all the Internet-connected things in your house and bring them together so that you can control them. It supports a long list of devices, including Nest thermostats, Samsung Smart Air Conditioners, Insteon LED Bulbs, Roku, Google Chromecast, Pebble smartwatches, Goji smart locks and much more. It's written in Node.js and can fit on a Raspberry Pi.

Middleware

IoTSyS

This IoT middleware provides a communication stack for smart devices. It supports multiple standards and protocols, including IPv6, oBIX, 6LoWPAN, Constrained Application Protocol and Efficient XML Interchange. Several videos on the website show how it works in action.

OpenIoT

The OpenIoT website explains that the project is "an open source middleware for getting information from sensor clouds, without worrying what exact sensors are used." It aims to enable cloud-based "sensing as a service," and has developed use cases for smart agriculture, intelligent manufacturing, urban crowdsensing, smart living and smart campuses.

AllJoyn

Originally created by Qualcomm, this open source operating system for the Internet of Things is now sponsored by one of the most prominent IoT organizations—The AllSeen Alliance, whose members include the Linux Foundation, Microsoft, LG, Qualcomm, Sharp, Panasonic, Cisco, Symantec and many others. It includes a framework and a set of services that will allow manufacturers to create compatible devices. It's cross-platform with APIs available for Android, iOS, OS X, Linux and Windows 7.

Contiki

Contiki describes itself as "the open source OS for the Internet of Things." It connects low-power microcontrollers to the internet and supports standards like IPv6, 6lowpan, RPL and CoAP. Other key features include highly efficient memory allocation, full IP networking, very low power consumption, dynamic module loading and more. Supported hardware platforms include Redwire Econotags,

Zolertia z1 motes, ST Microelectronics development kits and Texas Instruments chips and boards. Paid commercial support is available.

Raspbian

While the Raspberry Pi was intended as an educational device, many developers have begun using this credit-card-sized computer for IoT projects. The complete hardware specification is not open source, but much of the software and documentation is. Raspbian is a popular Raspberry Pi operating system that is based on the Debian distribution of Linux.

RIOT

RIOT bills itself as "the friendly operating system for the Internet of Things." Forked from the FeuerWhere project, RIOT debuted in 2013. It aims to be both developer- and resource-friendly. It supports multiple architectures, including MSP430, ARM7, Cortex-M0, Cortex-M3, Cortex-M4, and standard x86 PCs.

Spark

Spark is a distributed, cloud-based IoT operating system. The same company also offers easy-to-use hardware development kits and related products that start at just $39 (and the hardware designs are also open source). It includes a Web-based IDE, a command-line interface, support for multiple languages, and libraries for working with many different IoT devices. It has a very active user community, and a lot of documentation and online help are available.

Freeboard

Freeboard aims to let users create their own dashboards for monitoring IoT deployments. The code is freely available on GitHub or you can try the service for free if you make your dashboard public. Low-priced plans are also available for those who want to keep their data private. Sample dashboards oon the site show how they can be used to track air quality, residential appliances, distillery performance or environmental conditions in a humidor.

Exciting Printer

Exciting offers an open source kit for experimenting with IoT printing. It makes it possible to build your own small printer and use that printer to print out information obtained from various IoT devices. For example, it could print out a list of daily reminders, the weather report, *etc*. And in a interesting twist, if you want to contact the project owners, you can draw a picture that will be printed on the IoT printer in their office.

Platforms and Integration Tools

DeviceHive

It includes easy-to-use Web-based management software for creating networks, applying security rules and monitoring devices. The website offers sample projects built with DeviceHub, and it also has a "playground" section that allows users to use DeviceHub online to see how it works.

Devicehub.net

Devicehub.net describes itself as "the open source backbone for the Internet of Things." It's a cloud-based service that stores IoT-related data, provides visualizations of that data and allows users to control IoT devices from a Web page. Developers have used the service to create apps that track health information, monitor the location of children, automate household appliances, track vehicle data, monitor the weather and more.

IoT Toolkit

The group behind this project is working on a variety of tools for integrating multiple IoT-related sensor networks and protocols. The primary project is a Smart Object API, but the group is also working on an HTTP-to-CoAP Semantic mappin , an application framework with embedded software agents and more. They also sponsr a meetup group in Silicon Valley for people who are interested in IoT development.

Mango

Mango bills itself as "the world's most popular open source Machine-to-Machin (M2M) software." Web-based, it supports multiple platforms. Key features include support for multiple protocols and databases, meta points, user-defined events, import/export and more.

Nimbits

Nimbits can store and process a specific type of data—data that has been time- or geo-stamped. A public platform as a service is available, or you can download the software and deploy it on Google App Engine, any J2EE server on Amazon EC2 or on a Raspberry Pi. It supports multiple programming languages, including Arduino, JavaScript, HTML or the Nimbits.io Java library.

OpenRemote

OpenRemote offers four different integration tools for home-based hobbyists, integrators, distributors, and manufacturers. It supports dozens of different existing protocols, allowing users to create nearly any kind of smart device they can imagine and control it using any device that supports Java. The platform is open source, but the company also sells a wide variety of support, ebooks and other tools to aid in the design and product development process.

SiteWhere

SiteWhere is an open source IoT platform. It provides a system that facilitates the ingestion, storage, processing, and integration of device data. This project provides a complete platform for managing IoT devices, gathering data and integrating that data with external systems. Github

ThingSpeak

ThingSpeak can process HTTP requests and store and process data. Key features of the open data platform include an open API, real-time data collection, geolocation data, data processing and visualizations, device status messages and plugins. With ThingSpeak, the user can create sensor logging applications, location tracking applications, and a social network of things with status updates.

mnubo

mnubo is an SaaS solution providing a comprehensive Big Data platform catering to the Internet of Things via three solutions: mnubo smartobjects cloud, mnulabs and mnubo smartobjects analytics. Mnubo facilitates business logic modeling and Big Data analytics, speeding up your time to market by allowing you to focus on what you do best — building intelligent objects — with the mnubo platform providing the essential underlying technology support you need. It's the premier platform for Internet of Things developers to build, deploy and manage real world business rules and applications using machine data and derive advanced analytics and business insights for further innovation.

Key Features

- Deploy in public, private or hybrid cloud
- Build custom analytics, data-rich apps and business logic
- Handles large velocity, variety and volume of static data and IoT streams
- Descriptive, predictive, and prescriptive analytics
- Customized reporting
- Enhanced data visualizations
- Flexible APIs
- Reusable sensor templates
- Libraries and SDKs
- Sandbox environment access

Oracle

Oracle's Java Embedded solutions aim to reign in the massive amounts of data required for and created as a result of the Internet of Things by facilitating seamless communications between all elements of the IoT architecture. Delivering an integrated, secure and comprehensive platform for the entire IoT architecture across all vertical markets, Oracle enables real-time response and data capture from millions of device endpoints. Oracle offers several solutions, including Oracle Java SE Embedded, Oracle Java ME Embedded, Oracle Java Embedded Suite and Oracle Event Processing for Oracle Java Embedded to meet your specific technology requirements. Oracle Java SE Embedded is ideal for devices with 11 MB or more allocated storage for Java, while Oracle Java ME Embedded provides a feature-rich platform on devices lacking the resources necessary to run the full Java SE Embedded environment.

Key Features

- Real-time data capture
- Support millions of device endpoints

- Integrates with IT systems
- Lifecycle solution management
- M2M platform
- Proven middleware capabilities
- Facilitate communications between devices

Swarm

Swarm is an IoT development platform that facilitates adding new services to products easily. Swarm Dashboards serve as central, device-specific home pages, offering real-time, visual access to device features. Dashboards add value to connected products, enabling event notifications and alerts, historical data, analytics and reporting and other features for turning machine data into actionable insights. Swarm's parent company, Bug Labs, also provides Freeboard for building and deploying enterprise-class IoT applications and Dweet.io which is fittingly self-described as "Ridiculously simple data sharing for the Internet of Things."

Key Features

- Event notifications and alerts
- Real-time visualizations
- Analytics and reporting
- Integration with CRM/ERP products
- Historical activity logs
- Compliance testing
- Central device dashboards/customer portals
- Write device apps using standard web languages

Axeda

Axeda provides a comprehensive cloud-based platform for managing connected products and machines and implementing IoT and M2M applications. The platform is used to transform machine data into valuable insights, build and run applications and integrate machine data with other applications and systems to optimize business processes. Axeda's platform encompasses the full spectrum of developing and deploying applications and integrating M2M learning into everyday business processes, from preventative data security measures all the way to device provisioning and configuration.

Key Features

- Application services, integration framework and data management
- Integrate machine data into mission-critical applications
- Open API; REST and SOAP services
- 2-way, cloud-to-cloud communications

* Least cost routing
* Intelligent secure agents for internet, cellular and satellite
* Embedded agent toolkits
* Asset tracking and monitoring
* Alerts and notifications
* Device provisioning and configuration

OpenRemote

An open-source middleware solution for the Internet of Things, OpenRemote allows you to integrate any device — regardless of brand or protocol — and design any user interface for iOS, Android or web browsers. Using OpenRemote's cloud-based design tools for developing completely customized solutions, upgrades are streamlined, meaning your devices are literally future-proof.

Key Features

* Integrates a variety of protocols
* Customized solutions to suit your needs
* From single accounts to fully-branded solutions
* Cloud-based design tools

Etherios

Etherios is a comprehensive suite of products and services fully supporting connected enterprises. The Etherios Device Cloud is a PaaS solution enabling you to connect any product or device and gain real-time visibility into your assets. The Social Machine, Etherios' cloud-based SaaS solution, integrates machine data with your Salesforce.com instance, transforming it into actionable insights for deeper, more powerful CRM capabilities. With full services support for custom solutions and thousands of off-the-shelf wired and wireless solutions, Etherios bridges connectivity for the modern enterprise.

Key Features

* Off-the-shelf or custom solutions
* Cloud-enable any device with Cloud Connector
* State-of-the-art wireless lab
* Manage all connected devices from a single interface
* Monitor and control devices in real-time
* Secure and scalable infrastructure
* Secure multi-tenant, commercial-grade environment
* Integrate machine data with Salesforce via The Social Machine (SaaS)

ioBridge

Connect any product to a mobile device via the web with ioBridge's RealTime.io IoT platform and RealTime.io Iota technology. Whether you need to connect a single product or more than one million products, ioBridge speeds your time to market and lowers your cost per connected product. More than 50,000 users in 40 countries are already relying on ioBridge to Internet-able their devices, gather product usage data, perform remote device maintenance and gain real-time, actionable insights to drive decision-making.

Key Features

- ✯ Iota available as modules or firmware
- ✯ Simple installation
- ✯ Web API for custom applications
- ✯ Integrate with proprietary or third-party systems
- ✯ Free web-interface and user configurable dashboard
- ✯ Customers can create dashboards without writing software
- ✯ Supports 100,000 to 1,000,000 devices per server
- ✯ No subscriptions required for end users
- ✯ Iota-based gateway for off-the-shelf implementation

SAP Internet of Things Solutions

SAP's IoT solutions facilitate connectivity and multi-directional communication to enable users to interact with their devices in new ways. Transforming operations in field service and remote asset management, providing supply chain visibility and predicting and remedying logistics bottlenecks are just some of the challenges solved by SAP's remote maintenance and service, connected logistics and connected retail solutions for the IoT.

Key Features

- ✯ Integrate real-time data with distribution analytics
- ✯ Track and monitor assets
- ✯ Remotely update software
- ✯ Real-time, end-to-end visibility into freight, containers, shipped goods
- ✯ Identify and rectify logistics bottlenecks
- ✯ Real-time traffic control
- ✯ Gain insights into retail execution
- ✯ Respond to up-to-the-minute demand signals
- ✯ Use predictive algorithms for product-location optimization

Zatar

A new cloud-based infrastructure that automatically detects (or "sees") your devices and connects them to the Internet, Zatar is an open platform for managing your entire device network. By connecting all your devices to the same platform and facilitating M2M communication, all connected devices and their respective users can share data and collaborate seamlessly. Build new customer experiences or completely reinvent your business with Zatar's IoT and M2M platform.

Key Features

- User-friendly, tablet-optimized interface
- Cloud-based platform
- Out-of-the-box functionality; no development required
- Individual, device-specific profiles
- Real-time data visualization
- Public or private devices with shared access options
- Enables social media functions on IoT devices
- Works with all types of devices
- REST and JSON-based API
- Scalable
- Use off-the-shelf or custom apps

ThingWorx

ThingWorx facilitates rapid, streamlined creation of end-to-end smart applications for agriculture, cities, grid, water, building and telematics. Traditional industries are transformed and equipped with modern-day connectivity and smarter solutions through connected devices that provide comprehensive data collection and analysis for data-driven decision-making. ThingWorx reduces the time, cost and risks of building M2M and IoT applications. Users can build comprehensive mobile interfaces with zero coding, take advantage of ThingWorx Composer for application modeling, as well as real-time dashboards and collaborative workspaces — all with the scalability to support millions of devices.

Key Features

- Model-based design with ThingWorx Composer
- SQUEAL (Search, Query, Analysis) for search-based intelligence
- Complete design, runtime and intelligence environment
- Create real-time dashboards and collaborative workspaces
- Create mobile interfaces without coding
- Event-driven execution engine
- 3-dimensional storage
- Supports scale requirements for millions of devices
- Supports 3rd-party device clouds, direct network connections and more

Arrayent

Arrayent is an IoT platform for connected objects, enabling major brands like Whirlpool, Maytag and First Alert to bring smart, connected devices to consumers. The platform addresses both ends of the product spectrum with both enterprise and consumer apps, coupled with data analytics and a mobile framework for a complete plug-and-play installation at a reasonable cost. The platform scales to support millions of devices.

Key Features

- Arrayent Connect Cloud hosts virtual devices
- Complex application code resides in the cloud
- Email and SMS alerts
- iOS and Android push notifications
- Trigger response actions with alerts
- Over-the-air firmware downloads and updates
- 200-400ms end-to-end response times
- Device Protocol Interpreter (DPI) for legacy endpoint devices
- Supports a variety of computing platforms
- Consistent development interface across products

Sine-Wave Technologies

Sine-Wave Technologies is a premier Internet of Things platform enabling rapid development and deployment of high-performance, branded remote asset management solutions for enterprise companies. With a hosted set of APIs, the Sine-Wave Platform provides the support required to build, deploy and manage IoT applications. Hardware and network agnostic, Sine-Wave's open platform supports smart devices from any vendor as well as custom-built devices. You can even integrate with your legacy back-office systems using Sine-Wave's Business Adapter Framework.

Key Features

- Work with any network infrastructure
- Front-end API available via JavaScript/HTTP Servlet interface
- Develop applications using any modern computing language
- Device Adapter Framework written in Java or .NET
- Automatically scales for growth; no re-engineering required
- Interfaces for Transaction, Event, State and Trigger subsystems
- Cloud-hosted infrastructure
- Carrier-grade hosting platform
- Redundancy, failover and scaling without any changes to code base

- Business Adapter Framework to integrate legacy technologies
- Pay-as-you-grow licensing

Ayla Networks

A cloud-based application enablement platform, Ayla Networks is a simple and cost-effective solution for OEMs to connect any device to the Internet. With an adaptive fabric for building innovative applications that bridge communications between device, cloud and application, Ayla Networks provides powerful software agents embedded in both connected devices and mobile device applications for end-to-end support. With Ayla Networks, you can integrate secure connectivity and data intelligence into any product without significant design or business model modifications.

Key Features

- No need to re-architect host processor code
- Develop connected devices and apps in parallel
- Fully scalable
- Full over-the-air upgradeability
- Manage users, devices, and data with complete visibility
- Advanced application empowerment features
- User behavior analytics
- Cloud-cloud and cloud-enterprise APIs
- Multiple integration options
- Role-based permissions; multiple user types
- Device mapping
- Rules-based automation
- Schedule activities with user-defined on/off schedules

Echelon

Echelon is an Industrial Internet of Things (IIoT) platform with a full suite of chips, stacks, modules, interfaces and management software for developing devices, peer-to-peer communities and applications delivered via the IzoT Device Stack, IzoT Server Stack and FT 6000 EVK. Echelon is distinct from a consumer IoT platform [illegible]ddressing the core requirements for the IIoT, including autonomous control, [illegible] reliability, support for legacy evolution and exceptional security.

[illegible]ireless devices

[illegible]ters and management software

[illegible]hysical sensors and send to other devices

- REST APIs
- IzoT Python Package included in IzoT Device Stack
- Publish-subscribe data model over IP
- Ready-to-run software for Raspberry Pi
- Build myriad load control devices

EVRYTHNG

Give any product or object its own Active Digital Identity with the EVRYTHNG Engine, offering rich APIs, secure access and a persistent online presence. With EVRYTHNG, customers can personalize products with unique, user-generated digital content, brands can reward customers for actions or purchases, turn products into virtual objects to enable social sharing to drive sales, and access real-time analytics to capitalize on and improve upon the features and capabilities consumers demand. An end-to-end platform, EVRYTHNG provides everything you need for making products smart, interactive and trackable.

Key Features

- Serve millions of Active Digital Identities
- Persistent, unique digital presence for any physical object
- Object data exchange with CRMs or ERPs
- Supports a variety of technologies
- Control connected products directly from web
- Unique and re-programmable short URL for every object
- Powerful rules engine for personalized applications
- Organize products with collections, tags or batches
- Functional search
- HTTPS and crypto-secure API tokens
- Manage billions of objects without sacrificing performance

Exosite

Exosite enables developers to unlock the potential of Internet of Things applications with real-time, visual analytics and and scalable cloud device technologies. An end-to-end platform for building and deploying custom IoT applications, Exosite facilitates gaining valuable insights from everyday devices, empowering brands by putting their existing data at their fingertips in actionable form.

Key Features

- Hosted, server-based system
- Web service APIs
- Quickly prototype and deploy IoT apps

* Built-in framework eliminates infrastructure complexities
* Lightweight, flexible backend
* UDP, HTTP, JSON RPC, and Provisioning APIs
* Variety of Development Kits available

Xively

Xively, a LogMeIn product built on the Gravity Cloud, enables companies to leverage the Internet of Things to gain business insights from the physical world. Discover and deploy complete IoT solutions with the Xively IoT Platform, leverage innovations from Xively's world-class partner ecosystem and integrate your physical devices and associated data with your existing CRM, ERP or other business systems. Xively streamlines development with a PaaS model with searchable libraries of objects and permissions for dozens of languages and platforms, and Xively's RESTful API supports multiple data formats, including JSON, XML and CSV.

Key Features

* IoT Platform-as-a-Service built on public cloud
* Elastic scalability
* Intuitive lifecycle management capabilities
* Time-series archiving, conditional triggers and fine-grain permissions
* Device provisioning, activation and management
* Real-time message management and routing
* Developer Workbench and Device Management Console
* Supports millions of devices in real-time
* RESTful API supports JSON, XML & CSV data formats
* Client libraries for iOS, Android, JavaScript and more
* Server libraries for Ruby, Python, Java and more

Marvell

Marvell streamlines the process of bringing connected devices to the market with flexible and cost-effective solutions for OEMs and ODMs with both hardware and software solutions. Marvell's Wi-Fi Microcontroller Internet of Things Platform is a hardware/software platform enabling seamless connectivity with mobile clients, cloud services and other devices. Marvell's Avastar Wi-Fi SoCs feature firmware that performs much of the required Wi-Fi protocol handling, and the Easy-Connect Software is a feature-rich software stack for rapid development at a lower cost.

Key Features

* FreeRTOS Operating system
* Power management framework for low-power applications

- ★ Enable audio and visual streaming in any IoT device
- ★ Advanced networking middleware components
- ★ Built-in libraries to speed development
- ★ Built-in cloud and mobile client integrations
- ★ Flexible communications models for P2P, device-to-device
- ★ Over-the-air firmware upgrade support with minimal coding
- ★ Linux, Windows and MacOS development platform support

Carriots

Carriots is an IoT platform enabling companies to easily connect devices to the Internet and develop intelligent applications in just five steps. With two-way communication protocols, rule-based capabilities, and support for any device type, any hardware and Arduino, Raspberry Pi, Nanode and more, Carriots is a complete solution for quickly joining the IoT revolution.

Key Features

- ★ Apikeys, checksums and HTTPS
- ★ Data stored in NoSQL Big Data Base
- ★ RESTful API
- ★ Manage configurations and hardware remotely
- ★ If-then-else development approach
- ★ Groovy scripts; push and pull strategies
- ★ Integrate in external data flows or with other systems

Arkessa

Providing connectivity and management solutions for the IoT, Arkessa enables monitoring, management and control of connected devices with the same level of streamlined functionality as though your devices were connected directly to your desktop through its Mosaic IoT platform. Arkessa's Enterprise solutions empower companies to tap into the IoT to develop new revenue streams, improve customer satisfaction and deliver enhanced value from remote devices. Arkessa's platform is proven across more than 500 mobile networks spanning more than 200 countries around the globe.

Key Features

- ★ Available as a PaaS, leased or licensed solution
- ★ Hosted in-cloud, in-data-center or on-premise
- ★ Compatible with new IoT devices or legacy M2M devices
- ★ Real-time control and consolidated data
- ★ Single estate management portal for device management

- Oracle-certified as ExaStack Ready
- Integrate machine data with CRM, ERP, big data and analytics systems
- Fully encrypted data complies with international regulations
- Supports GSM, GPRS, 3G, 4G, and satellite

GroveStreams

From energy to health care to business, GroveStreams offers IoT solutions for a multitude of industries, including sensor technology for environmental monitoring. GroveStreams' patent-pending data streaming analytics platform enables you to collect massive amounts of data and analyze in real-time to drive smarter decision-making.

Key Features

- Can store over 60 million data points
- Supports many data types
- Accurate sample times to the millisecond
- Derived streams
- Interval gap detection for data quality monitoring
- Drag-and-drop HTML dashboard
- Role-based access security
- RESTful API
- Time-of-use filtering

CeNSE by HP

HP is revolutionizing the way data is gathered and analyzed with CeNSE (Central Nervous System for the Earth). It's a highly-intelligent network consisting of billions of nanoscale sensors capable of taste, smell, vision, touch and hearing. Providing real-time data on the physical environment, CeNSE enables businesses and organizations to detect and respond better to environmental, biological and physical or structural changes. The first commercial application of CeNSE technology is being conducted with Shell, which will entail a wireless sensing system to acquire high-resolution seismic data for a clear picture of oil and gas reservoirs.

Key Features

- Sensors will be able to detect gas leaks and other issues
- Useful for roads, buildings and other infrastructure
- Potential use for detecting food/water contamination
- Useful for disease control and patient monitoring
- Could lead to 10x gains in production
- Could extend the life of manufacturing components by 50%

ARM

ARM creates sensors, controllers, microprocessors and other types of embedded intelligence for the IoT, enabling ordinary objects to automatically sense variables in the environment, communicate with other devices and objects and interact with cloud-based applications and other networks. ARM licenses technology to various partners, enabling organizations to add value and differentiate themselves from competitors.

Key Features

- ✯ Cortex processors
- ✯ Develop high-performance, low-cost platforms
- ✯ Processors handle multiple I/O channels and protocol standards
- ✯ Keli Tools
- ✯ PIPD ultra low-leakage libraries
- ✯ Graphics processors and video engines
- ✯ Smart cards, smart meters and other embedded products
- ✯ Peripherals and development tools; DS-5 Development Studio

Nimbits

Nimbits is aPaaS that can be downloaded on a Raspberry Pi, Web Server, Amazon EC2, or Google App Engine. The platform is used for developing hardware and software solutions that can connect to the cloud or to each other, logging and retrieving large amounts of data from physical devices, triggering events or alerts, or initiating complex analysis.

Key Features

- ✯ Download Nimbits servers on chips, servers or the cloud
- ✯ Open-source platform
- ✯ Event triggers and alerts
- ✯ Record and process geo and time-stamped data
- ✯ Build provided for Google App Engine and Linux Systems
- ✯ Compatible with most J2EE servers (Apache Tomcat, Jetty Server)

Open Sen.se

Open Sen.se doesn't address the Internet of Things, but the Internet of Everything — a world in which humans, nature, machines, information, objects and environments all interact and communicate in different ways. Open Sen.se provides a platform for imagining, prototyping and testing new devices, installations, scenarios and applications for this new interconnected world. It's both free and easy to use, enabling both professionals and amateur hobbyists to experiment with ease.

Key Features

- Turn information into action with triggers
- Devices, humans and applications post data to Sen.se
- Real-time interaction with remote devices and objects
- Rich visualizations
- Mashup tools

Paraimpu

Paraimpu is a social tool for connecting physical and virtual devices, composing and interconnecting them and sharing data and published objects on the social web. Using Paraimpu, you can create customized applications for the Internet of Things, enabling your devices and objects to react to environmental changes, activities or events. Ultimately, the result is a physical-virtual web mashup in which users can tap into shared data and virtual objects to further their own applications and devices.

Key Features

- Connect things, services, devices and APIs
- Link things together or connect to social networks
- Set rules and triggers
- Easy-to-use facilities for Max/MSP
- Pre-defined Things categories
- Create and manage things-based applications
- Connect up to 8 things
- 43,200 communications per month
- 500 data items per thing stored in the cloud

Sociot.al

Sociot.al is a project focused on creating a socially aware, citizen-centric Internet of Things. Today, the IoT is heavily business-centric, with enterprise applications being used to optimize business processes and extract real-world knowledge from environments. In these systems, the data is available only within a pre-defined network or space. Sociot.al aims to bridge the gap between these enterprise, business-centric IoT systems and citizen provided infrastructure, facilitating open eco-systems in which data and information are shared freely and securely. An ongoing, in-the-works project, Sociot.al has a clear workplan and vision for enabling a citizen-centric IoT.

Key Features

Proposed tools and workplan to lower barriers of citizen participation in IoT:

- Simple, intuitive user environment
- API for device integration

* Simple service creation capabilities
* Plugins for most common platforms
* Service creation environment for developers
* Professional and citizen contributions

Piloting 2 services in Santander and Novi Sad:

* Public safety
* Resource efficiency

NewAer

NewAer's proximity platform SDK is a lightweight, low-power client for making apps contextually-aware without beacons. It works across all types of devices and platforms, works equally well both inside and outside, and is capable of triggering actions both in-device or in-cloud. NewAer also offers three applications: Share, for exchanging files between nearby devices, Kiosk, enabling proximity advertising without the use of beacons, and ToothTag, for setting actions and customizations without pairing by simply tagging devices.

Key Features

* Build apps for all types of devices
* No extra hardware
* Enables communication between any platforms
* Use anything as a beacon
* No pairing necessary; utilizes radio technology
* All radios interact rather than existing in parallel
* Path rules to applications
* Low power

SensorCloud

SensorCloud is a solution from LORD MicroStrain, a company that produces smart, embedded transducers, sensors and sensor networks. SensorCloud provides integrated Big Data analytics, automated alerts and actionable reports for predictive maintenance and streamlined monitoring of connected devices. A unique data storage, virtualization and remote management platform, SensorCloud supports any device, sensor or sensor network through an OpenData API.

Key Features

* Unlimited data storage
* Triple-redundant reliability
* Collect and preserve long-term sensor data streams
* Time series visualization/graphing tool
* Easily navigate through vast amounts of data

- Drill down to singular points of interest
- Quickly deploy data processing and analysis apps
- Flexible SMS/email alert scripting

ThingSpeak

An open data platform for the Internet of Things, ThingSpeak enables real-time data collection with an Open API and sophisticated data processing and analysis capabilities. With plugins, data visualizations and the ability to integrate your data with a variety of third-party platforms, systems and technologies, including other leading IoT platforms such as ioBridge and Arduino, ThingSpeak is the perfect complement to an existing enterprise system to tap into the Internet of Things.

Key Features

- Open API
- Integrate with Raspberry Pi, Adruino, ioBridge/RealTime.io and more
- Geo-location data
- Data processing and visualizations
- Device status messages
- Social network integration
- Integrations with data analytics and third-party services
- ThingSpeak API powered by Phusion Passenger Enterprise

Yaler

Yaler provides a relay infrastructure providing secure Web and SSH access to embedded systems, even if they're located behind a firewall, NAT or mobile network router, and it works with any device with a TCP socket. A pay-per-use platform, Yaler is a cost-effective solution offering premium enterprise support. Examples are provided in C, C#, Java and Python for use with Raspberry Pi, Arduino, Netduino, BeagleBone and similar devices.

Key Features

- Plug-and-play functionality for end users
- Access via any browser or phone
- Addressability and accessibility for devices blocked by firewalls, NAT or mobile routers
- Access your device from a client such as a browser, Curl, Android, *etc*.

Cost: Contact for a quote

Jasper

Jasper is used by some of the world's largest corporations to launch, manage and monetize connected devices and powerful IoT applications. The highly-configurable Jasper Control Board Platform is customizable to suit your specific operational needs, business models and requirements across all industries and around the world. Jasper serves IoT needs such as connected cars and enterprise mobility, offering full network visibility across all devices and real-time monitoring for precise control and deeper insights to drive decision-making.

Key Features

- ✯ Automate and control devices
- ✯ Analyze behavior patterns and performance
- ✯ Real-time monitoring
- ✯ Configure rules for segmentation and scoring
- ✯ Set up offers, campaigns and programs
- ✯ Define service alerts and campaign events
- ✯ Maintain full network visibility
- ✯ Automate activation processes
- ✯ Real-time issue identification and troubleshooting
- ✯ Integrates with existing IT infrastructure

XobXob

Add any project to the IoT with XobXob's simple cloud service. Connected devices can send and receive messages from Xobs, which function as small mailboxes. By sharing Xobs, devices can communicate and interact with each other, enabling actions such as the remote control of a garage door using a smartphone. Designed to be simple with minimal programming required, XobXob provides a range of sample projects and tools to streamline the process.

Key Features

- ✯ Connects physical and virtual devices
- ✯ RESTful API
- ✯ Works with any platform connected to the Internet
- ✯ Arduino libraries
- ✯ Currently in Alpha phase
- ✯ Additional libraries and sample projects to be itnroduced

Linkafy

Linkafy empowers the smart home with a PaaS for appliance manufacturers to easily introduce connected appliances to the market. Linkafy serves as a single application that can control all appliances in the end user's home or environment, rather than the complex myriad of apps generally required to operate multiple devices from different manufacturers. Manufacturers use Linkafy's API or SDK to integrate with IoT-ready devices, enabling customers to control, monitor and schedule tasks on multiple home appliances from a central interface.

Key Features

- ✯ View appliance notifications in a central interface
- ✯ Handle notifications and schedule tasks remotely
- ✯ Share remote control and monitoring with other users
- ✯ Monitor utilities consumption over time
- ✯ Notifications based on events and triggers
- ✯ Configure daily schedules for security monitoring or other actions
- ✯ Works across all mobile platforms

Revolv

Unify, control and automate all of your smart home appliances and connected devices with Revolv. A future-proofed system with 7 radios and compatibility with hundreds of devices, Revolv is a simple and seamless solution for end consumers to make sense and take control over the IoT.

Key Features

- ✯ Home or remote control of lights, appliances
- ✯ Connect to the Hub via local Wi-Fi
- ✯ No Ethernet cable required
- ✯ Flash Link™ technology uses smartphone camera flash to transfer data
- ✯ Central 'Home' Dashboard offers birds-eye view of all devices
- ✯ Set up device-to-device automated actions
- ✯ Geo-Sense, Time-Based, Device-to-Device, On-Demand actions

Wind River

Wind River has been providing connected intelligence of the IoT-caliber for decades. Wind River provides a foundation for the reliable and efficient operation of IoT networks and connected devices for highly-regulated industries and mission-critical applications.

Key Features

- ✯ Connect legacy devices to the IoT
- ✯ Manage sensor data
- ✯ Real-time monitoring and analysis
- ✯ Powers sophisticated applications for automotive, aerospace and more
- ✯ Converge siloed systems

Wovyn

An open, distributed architecture for delving into new opportunities and business models with the IoT, Wovyn is capable of connecting any sensor to any app using any protocol. Used for personal, commercial, industrial and military applications, Wovyn is a powerful middleware platform for the Internet of Things.

Key Features

- ★ Wireless sensors for real-time monitoring
- ★ Configure notifications via SMS, Text or Email
- ★ Wi-Fi, 2G and 3G Connectivity
- ★ Flexible platform
- ★ Wovyn USB and Wi-Fi sensor products

Microsoft Research Lab of Things

A platform for experimental research, Microsoft Research's Lab of Things is an innovative solution enabling the interconnection of devices and implementation of application scenarios. Enterprises can deploy and monitor field studies and analyze experimental data, as well as share data, code and participants among a connected, cooperative community. Projects span healthcare, energy management, home automation and other sectors, supporting large numbers of sensors and devices at scale.

Key Features

- ★ Deploy sensors and devices
- ★ HomeOS client side component/source code platform
- ★ HomeOS deployed on Windows-based PC (HomeHub)
- ★ Experiments are deployed from HomeHubs
- ★ Apps and source code samples
- ★ Alerts, Camera Viewer, Sensor, Lights apps
- ★ Deploy off-the-shelf or custom devices

InfoBright

InfoBright helps enterprises to compete based on analytical maturity with its Knowledge Grid architecture that serves as an analytical database platform for the Internet of Things, empowering businesses to store, analyze and act upon vast amounts of machine-generated data. With a free community edition and an enterprise-class version for companies requiring robust performance and capabilities, InfoBright is compatible with leading Business Intelligence platforms such as Cognos and Microstrategy, facilitating fully interconnected business systems.

Key Features

- ★ No specific schemas required
- ★ Compatible with Business Intelligence platforms (Pentaho, Talend, Jaspersoft, *etc.*)
- ★ Query and load performance remain constant with database growth

- ✯ Distributed Load Processor for loading TBs per hour
- ✯ Scales to handle petrabytes of data
- ✯ No complex hardware infrastructure required
- ✯ Runs on industry-standard, low-cost servers
- ✯ Each server can scale to process hundreds of tetrabytes of data
- ✯ 10:1 to 40:1 data compression
- ✯ Fast response times for complex ad-hoc queries

Contiki

Contiki is an open-source operating system for the Internet of Things, connecting low-cost, low-power microcontrollers to the Internet and enabling rapid, streamlined development. Instant Contiki provides an entire development environment in a single download, and applications are written in standard C. The Cooja simulator Contiki networks can be emulated before burned into hardware; Contiki runs on a range of low-power wireless devices — most of which can be purchased easily via the Internet. There are a variety of hardware platforms available for free within the Contiki code.

Key Features

- ✯ Highly memory efficient
- ✯ Memory allocation mechanisms (memm, memb, *etc.*)
- ✯ Full IP network stack
- ✯ Designed for extremely low-power systems
- ✯ Supports standardized standardized IETF protocols
- ✯ ContikiMAC radio duty cycling mechanism enables sleepy routers
- ✯ Coffee, lightweight flash file system
- ✯ Optional command-line shell
- ✯ Rime wireless networking stack
- ✯ Cooja simulator for emulating hardware devices

2lemetry

2lemetry powers the connected enterprise, transforming raw data into real-time actionable intelligence by interconnecting people, devices and data. Functioning similar to an Enterprise Application Integration (EAI) middleware solution, the 2lemetry ThingFabric platform provides scaled device connectivity, cross communication and data brokerage and storage. But 2lemetry doesn't stop with data collection, providing predictive computational models and a configurable rules engine for enabling automation and gaining actionable intelligence.

Key Features

- ✯ Hardware agnostic

- Small device client footprint
- No database design or complex device configuration required
- Auto-provisioning
- Makes data immediately available in local business applications
- No minimum or maximum device limits
- Capable of storing billions of records per customer (petrabytes of data)
- Instant read-write capabilities even for major Big Data loads
- ISO 270001 compliant, with partners completing SAS70 Type II audit

AllJoyn

AllJoyn enables compatible smart devices within proximity to recognize one another, communicate and share data across brands, networks and operating systems. Initially developed by Qualcomm Innovation Center, Inc., AllJoyn is now an open-source project of the AllSeen Alliance, providing a common central language to support the Internet of Things and empowering developers and manufacturers with the tools and technologies they need for forward-thinking IoT innovation.

Key Features

- Powerful engine enabling P2P experiences
- Proximal peer connectivity
- Reduce time, effort and cost of adding P2P capabilities to apps
- Supports a variety of operating systems
- Optimized for mobile
- High performance; low latency

InterDigital

Developing fundamental enabling technologies for M2M communications and facilitating a common framework and roadmap for cellular operators, service providers and device manufacturers, InterDigtial is centered around a standard service layer and API. Both are independent, network- and application-aware, fully enabling manufacturers and developers to harness the potential of M2M communications. InterDigital has been contributing to the IoT standardization process since 2009, building pioneering prototypes and demonstrations to support the emerging oneM2M global standard.

Key Features

- Adaptable to emerging oneM2M global standard
- Network agnostic
- Removes dependency on proprietary technology solutions
- Enables development of M2M and IoT applications across verticals
- Configurable, easy-to-use SDK

- Greatly reduced CAPEX and OPEX; re-use service packages
- Standardized Service Delivery Platform (SDP)
- Minimizes M2M/IoT traffic in the core network
- Set of common APIs for scalable/horizontal M2M and IoT services
- Integrate multiple applications and manage entire ecosystems

Superflux Internet of Things Academy (IoTA)

Design and research lab Superflux is working on an ongoing project commissioned by Sony to experiment with building IoTA, an open, educational Internet-of-Things platform to encourage innovation and creativity and enhance technological literacy. It's a part of Sony's Futurescapes project in collaboration with Forum for the Future, first a proposed concept that has now evolved to the investigation of actually developing the proposed model. A film documents the experience to date, conducted in conjunction with Forum for the Future and Technology Will Save Us. The project is currently in talks with potential partners with the goal of developing experience prototypes.

Key Features

- Currently in investigation phase
- Pilot project at Oasis Academy in Manchester
- Goals:
  - Balance accessibility with complexity to encourage broad use
  - Adaptable to grow with vast amounts of user-generated content
  - Well-connected with networks and companies outside the Academy
- Dedicated design and experience prototyping phase next

HarvestGeek

HarvestGeek is an excellent example of an innovative IoT application in real-world use. HarvestGeek enables sustainable agriculture with smart technology that builds sensors into gardens and crops, providing essential data on temperature, light, moisture and other conditions that impact plant growth. Data can be used to trigger automated actions, meaning users can control equipment to rectify environmental conditions to maximize yield.

Key Features

- Monitor conditions remotely and in real-time
- Detect and rectify problems
- Log data for detailed review and analysis
- Create customized alerts
- Automate greenhouse operations
- Open-source platform

MediaTek Labs

MediaTek Labs is a developer-centric ecosystem supporting device creation, application development and services surrounding MediaTek's other products and services. A provider of system-on-chip (SoC) solutions, MediaTek Labs is a central hub for all MediaTek developer and creator offerings, including SDKs, HDKs, technical documentation and support. Recently, the company introduced MediaTek LinkIt, a platform enabling the development of wearable devices and IoT applications.

Key Features

- MediaTek Aster, the smallest SoC for wearable devices
- Reference designs for various form factors, functionalities and connected services
- Software architecture modularity
- Plug-in SDKs for Arduino and VisualStudio
- Supports over-the-air updates for apps, algorithms and drivers

Streamlite LTE

Sequan's product line for the connected devices market, Streamlite LTE provides both functionality and throughput to empower cost-effective IoT devices. The Colibri LTE platform is the core Streamlite LTE offering, delivering an ideal set of IoT-compatible features for high efficiency and cost-effective solutions. Suitable for adding connectivity to to M2M and IoT modules, Colibri LTE provides a comprehensive software package for over-the-air device management.

Key Features

- Throughput up to Category 4
- Sequans AIR™ interference cancellation technology
- Android, ChromeOS, Linux, Windows, MAC OS host environments
- Enhanced, integrated network and application CPU
- Carrier-proven LTE protocol stack
- Suitable for designing tablets, CPE, mobile routers, PCs, residential gateways and more

Bosch Software Innovations Suite

The Bosch Software Innovations Suite is modular for advanced flexibility, enabling device management, business process management, and business rules management for the IoT. It integrates seamlessly with existing IT infrastructures for streamlined connectivity and enhanced data analytics. The Bosch Software Innovations Suite is powering the IoT by connecting the four key elements of the ecosystem: People (Users) , Things, Enterprises and Partners.

Key Features

- Modular system
- Quick, easy integration with IT systems
- Process, rule and device management
- Proven technology
- Improve existing projects
- Initiate new business models
- Deployed in 600+ international projects

RIoTboard

RIoTboard is revolutionizing the Internet of Things with its open-source platform serving demanding applications that require high levels of processing power. It's an open-source board with detailed schematics downloadable for use in any design, and it offers an Android OS distribution for applications requiring tablet or mobile experiences, as well as a Linux download.

Key Features

- Peripherals, expandability and processor power
- Freescale i.MX 6Solo applications processor
- ARM Cortex-A9 architecture
- Sophisticated graphics and video processing capabilities
- Freescale's Kinetis MCU (K20) MCU integration
- Variety of interfaces and connectivity options

5

IoT Applications for a Smarter World

SMART CITIES

Smart Parking

Monitoring of parking spaces availability in the city.

Structural Health

Monitoring of vibrations and material conditions in buildings, bridges and historical monuments.

Noise Urban Maps

Sound monitoring in bar areas and centric zones in real time.

Smartphone Detection

Detect iPhone and Android devices and in general any device which works with WiFi or Bluetooth interfaces.

Eletromagnetic Field Levels

Measurement of the energy radiated by cell stations and and WiFi routers.

Traffic Congestion

Monitoring of vehicles and pedestrian levels to optimize driving and walking routes.

Smart Lighting

Intelligent and weather adaptive lighting in street lights.

Waste Management

Detection of rubbish levels in containers to optimize the trash collection routes.

Smart Roads

Intelligent Highways with warning messages and diversions according to climate conditions and unexpected events like accidents or traffic jams.

SMART ENVIRONMENT

Forest Fire Detection

Monitoring of combustion gases and preemptive fire conditions to define alert zones.

Air Pollution

Control of CO_2 emissions of factories, pollution emitted by cars and toxic gases generated in farms.

Snow Level Monitoring

Snow level measurement to know in real time the quality of ski tracks and allow security corps avalanche prevention.

Landslide and Avalanche Prevention

Monitoring of soil moisture, vibrations and earth density to detect dangerous patterns in land conditions.

Earthquake Early Detection

Distributed control in specific places of tremors.

SMART WATER

Potable Water Monitoring

Monitor the quality of tap water in cities.

Chemical Leakage Detection in Rivers

Detect leakages and wastes of factories in rivers.

Swimming pool remote measurement

Control remotely the swimming pool conditions.

Pollution levels in the sea

Control realtime leakages and wastes in the sea.

Water Leakages

Detection of liquid presence outside tanks and pressure variations along pipes.

River Floods

Monitoring of water level variations in rivers, dams and reservoirs.

SMART METERING

Smart Grid

Energy consumption monitoring and management.

Tank level

Monitoring of water, oil and gas levels in storage tanks and cisterns.

Photovoltaic Installations

Monitoring and optimization of performance in solar energy plants.

Water Flow

Measurement of water pressure in water transportation systems.

Silos Stock Calculation

Measurement of emptiness level and weight of the goods.

SECURITY & EMERGENCIES

Perimeter Access Control

Access control to restricted areas and detection of people in non-authorized areas.

Liquid Presence

Liquid detection in data centers, warehouses and sensitive building grounds to prevent break downs and corrosion.

Radiation Levels

Distributed measurement of radiation levels in nuclear power stations surroundings to generate leakage alerts.

Explosive and Hazardous Gases

Detection of gas levels and leakages in industrial environments, surroundings of chemical factories and inside mines.

RETAIL

Supply Chain Control

Monitoring of storage conditions along the supply chain and product tracking for traceability purposes.

NFC Payment

Payment processing based in location or activity duration for public transport, gyms, theme parks, *etc.*

Intelligent Shopping Applications

Getting advices in the point of sale according to customer habits, preferences, presence of allergic components for them or expiring dates.

Smart Product Management

Control of rotation of products in shelves and warehouses to automate restocking processes.

LOGISTICS

Quality of Shipment Conditions

Monitoring of vibrations, strokes, container openings or cold chain maintenance for insurance purposes.

Item Location

Search of individual items in big surfaces like warehouses or harbours.

Storage Incompatibility Detection

Warning emission on containers storing inflammable goods closed to others containing explosive material.

Fleet Tracking

Control of routes followed for delicate goods like medical drugs, jewels or dangerous merchandises.

INDUSTRIAL CONTROL

M2M Applications

Machine auto-diagnosis and assets control.

Indoor Air Quality

Monitoring of toxic gas and oxygen levels inside chemical plants to ensure workers and goods safety.

Temperature Monitoring

Control of temperature inside industrial and medical fridges with sensitive merchandise.

Ozone Presence

Monitoring of ozone levels during the drying meat process in food factories.

Indoor Location

Asset indoor location by using active (ZigBee) and passive tags (RFID/NFC).

Vehicle Auto-diagnosis

Information collection from CanBus to send real time alarms to emergencies or provide advice to drivers.

SMART AGRICULTURE

Wine Quality Enhancing

Monitoring soil moisture and trunk diameter in vineyards to control the amount of sugar in grapes and grapevine health.

Green Houses

Control micro-climate conditions to maximize the production of fruits and vegetables and its quality.

Golf Courses

Selective irrigation in dry zones to reduce the water resources required in the green.

Meteorological Station Network

Study of weather conditions in fields to forecast ice formation, rain, drought, snow or wind changes.

Compost

Control of humidity and temperature levels in alfalfa, hay, straw, *etc.* to prevent fungus and other microbial contaminants.

SMART ANIMAL FARMING

Hydroponics

Control the exact conditions of plants grown in water to get the highest efficiency crops.

Offspring Care

Control of growing conditions of the offspring in animal farms to ensure its survival and health.

Animal Tracking

Location and identification of animals grazing in open pastures or location in big stables.

Toxic Gas Levels

Study of ventilation and air quality in farms and detection of harmful gases from excrements.

DOMESTIC & HOME AUTOMATION

Energy and Water Use

Energy and water supply consumption monitoring to obtain advice on how to save cost and resources.

Remote Control Appliances

Switching on and off remotely appliances to avoid accidents and save energy.

Intrusion Detection Systems

Detection of windows and doors openings and violations to prevent intruders.

Art and Goods Preservation

Monitoring of conditions inside museums and art warehouses.

EHEALTH

Fall Detection

Assistance for elderly or disabled people living independent.

Medical Fridges

Control of conditions inside freezers storing vaccines, medicines and organic elements.

Sportsmen Care

Vital signs monitoring in high performance centers and fields.

Patients Surveillance

Monitoring of conditions of patients inside hospitals and in old people's home.

Ultraviolet Radiation

Measurement of UV sun rays to warn people not to be exposed in certain hours.

6

Useful Resources For IoT Professional

1. Alasdair Allas: Workshops on Sensors

Allas offers his iOS sensors and external hardware masterclass. This is one of our favorite workshops on sensors. Done well, you'll be able to make basic location aware applications for the iOS platforms. You'll be using onboard sensors: the 3-axis accelerometer, the magnetometer, the gyroscope, the camera and the GPS. Allas has also authored a book titled Learning iOS Programming. Anyone looking to hack their way into iOS based IoT apps can attend the upcoming workshops at London, San Francisco, and New York.

2. Lynda: IoT with Android

Those of you who are interested in developing Android based IoT apps can check Michael Lehman's course on Lynda. You'll come to know how to use IFTTT to program things, creating your own things with programmable hardware & how to connect inputs and outputs. Michael offers IoT courses for both Android & iOS, he has been with Microsoft's Patterns & Practices and Developer/Platform Evangelism groups and now runs his Seattle based consulting firm DreamTimeStudioZ, LLC.

3. Lynda: IoT with iOS

The Lynda course on IoT teaches programmers how to program the internet of things with iOS. You'll get to know all things wireless and communication networks that can be used in IoT projects.

4. Microsoft: Cross-platform development in IoT

This course by Microsoft Channel 9 allows attendees to see how easily they can create solutions using Windows IoT "Athens" on mobile and industry devices.

5. Microsoft: IoT Mobile Apps

This course at Microsoft Virtual Academy delves deep into 'how-to' of building

IoT Mobile Apps. The course is 50 minutes of video tutorial and also address the scalability issue often reported in IoT mobile apps.

6. Rockwell Automation: Industrial Ethernet

Essentials of Industrial Ethernet Networks for an OT Professional by Rockwell Automation. This is 2 day course, and a prerequisite to attending the course is your ability to perform basic Windows® operating system tasks. The guys there will make you hands-on in IoT exercises by performing on an EtherNet/IP™ workstation and/or use a variety of software tools. The course is aimed towards OT (operations technology) professionals but with IoT, it is never a bad idea to know plenty of stuff right from devices to the integration, services and dashboard layer.

7. Telecoms Academy: Connected Devices

This one is a bit expensive 2 day course (Early Bird – £1035 Sep 29-30, 2015) around networking technologies for application within IoT projects. The course also aims to educate participants for applying effective techniques to utilize agents in creating IoT projects.

8. NFC: Certification for IoT products

NFC forum offers a certification for near-field-communication products used within the IoT projects. The course highlights the specifications that must be implemented by a device to be eligible to receive the NFC Forum Certification Mark.

9. ARC Chart: Radio Technologies for IoT

The two day course by ARC Chart will teach you some nerdy stuff about radio spectrum, IoT allocations, ISM bands, and cognitive radio techniques. You'll learn some meshing techniques and new networks that have emerged such as Sigfox, LoRA, Weightless. The course is targeted words a broad range of technical and business persons. Again, it is in London (and expensive around £945 for two days course.

10. Big Data Trainings: Experfy

With some programming and statistics problem solving experience, this Experfy course revolves around Neural Networks, Machine Learning System Design, Clustering Anomaly Detection and recommendation system design. This course is only available for on-site for corporate training on days and location that is convenient to your team.

Since, Big Data becomes an inevitable part of the larger IoT projects, it is good to have a good handle over Hadoop and other big data technologies.

11. RapidStart: Certified IoT Specialist

The Singapore based RapidStart offers this IoT specialist certification comprising 40 hours of course spanning over 5 days.The good thing about this course is that it also includes Big Data modules.

12. Noble Prog: IoT for Executives

Anyone whose new to IoT and feels inadequate in electronics & devices layer of IoT should check this resource. Noble Prog course on IoT covers a good deal of electronics stuff involved in typical IoT projects. By far it is one of the most comprehensive IoT course out there on the web. Let us know if a course beats this in detail to each layer in a typical IoT solution

13. Rockwell Automation: Industrial IoT

Rockwell's name has become synonymous with some good early-adopted IoT projects. This course is for IT professionals with limited background of industrial automation and control on IP (Internet Protocol) networks used in industrial settings. A good course if you really look forward to establishing yourself in the IoT enterprise space.

14. Blackhat USA: IoT Security

If you are someone who keeps dreading about security issues of IoT devices and solutions, this is a must-attend event by Blackhat USA. Although, the event was scheduled for July this year, you can still get hold of their proceedings and presentations. The event has extensively covered issues such as hardware & software debugging, web and mobile based vulnerabilities, identifying attack surfaces and white fuzzers and how to bypass security mitigation. The all-in-one nerdy-nifty security & privacy related event for IoT & M2M practitioners.

15. Tonex: Internet of Things Training

The Texas based Tonex (Technology & Mgmt Training course provider) offers IoT training for a whopping sum of $1999.00 The course covers the four layers of an IoT solution (connectivity, integration, services and visualization), especially the connectivity methods & technologies are given a fair share in this course (wireless 101, RF 101, ZigBee, RFID, Bluetooth LE or Bluetooth Smart Technology, IEEE 802.15.4, IEEE 802.15.4e, 802.11ah). Considering the price tag of this training course, only the one who has attanded the session can opine that how much is it worth spending the amount (please comment if anyone knows how well Tonex delivers this training).

16. Cisco: Industrial Networking Specialist

Cisco is to networking as Apple is to smartphone. The industrial networking courses by Cisco can make you well-versed in OSI layers of IP networks, as well as networking devices like routers and switches, and cabling approaches; specific industrial devices such as drives, PLCs, sensors, and substation equipment; relevant industrial standards and models such as TIA, the Purdue model, and environmental standards; and various safety protocols important in an industrial zone (Cisco). The three courses specifically designed around industrial internet & networking can make you a networking ninga.

17. Award Solutions: The World of IoT

The Texas based training & services provider, Award Solutions, offers instructor-led courses on IP and the Internet, Iot & Big Data and security of IoT environments, and specific application of IoT in business world.

7

Testing IoT

IoT Test Approaches

#1) Usability

- We need to make sure the usability of each of the device used here.
- The medical healthcare tracking device used should be portable enough to be moved into different segments of the medical.
- The equipment should be smart enough to push not only the notifications but also the error messages, warnings *etc.*
- The system should have an option to log all the events to provide clarity to the end users. If it is not capable of doing that, the system should push those as well to a database to store it.
- The notifications should be shown and handling of the display should be done properly in the devices [computers/mobile devices].
- Usability in terms of displaying data, processing data, pushing job tasks from the devices should be tested thoroughly.

#2) IoT Security

- IoT Security challenges: IoT is data centric where all the devices/system connected operate based on the data that is available.
- When it comes to the data flow between devices, there is always a chance that the data can be accessed or read when getting transferred.
- From a testing standpoint, we need to check if the data is protected/ encrypted when getting transferred from one device to the other.
- Wherever, there is an UI, we need to make sure there is a password protection on it.

3) Connectivity

- As it is a healthcare solution, connectivity plays a vital role.

- ★ The system has to be available all the time and should have seamless connectivity with the stakeholders.
- ★ As per connectivity, two things are very important to test;
  - Connectivity, transfer of data, receiving job tasks from the devices should be seamless when the connection is UP and running.
  - The other condition is the connection down scenario. Doesn't matter how robust is the system and the network, there are chances that the system will go offline. Being a tester, we should test the offline conditions as well. Once the system is not available on the network, there has to be an alert which can prompt the physicians so that they can start to monitor the health conditions manually not depending on the system till it is up. On the other hand, there has to be a mechanism in the system which can store all the data in it during the offline period. Once the system comes online, all that data should get propagated. Data loss should not be there in any condition.

#4) Performance

- ★ When we are talking about a system for a healthcare domain, we need to make sure the system is scalable enough for the whole hospital.
- ★ When the testing is carried out, it is done for 2-10 patients at a time and the data is propagated to 10-20 devices.
- ★ When the whole hospital is connected and 180-200 patients are connected to the system, the data that is propagated is much bigger than the tested data.
- ★ As testers, we need to make sure the system performs the same even though the added data is propagated.
- ★ We should also test the monitoring utility to display the system usage, power usage, temperature *etc.*

#5) Compatibility Testing

- ★ Looking at the complex architecture of an IoT system, compatibility testing is a must.
- ★ Testing items such as, multiple operating system versions, browser types and respective versions, generations of devices, communication modes [For e.g. Bluetooth 2.0, 3.0] is necessary for IoT compatibility testing.

#6) Pilot Testing

- ★ As far as the IoT is concerned, Pilot testing is a must.
- ★ Only testing in Lab makes sure the product/system works fine. But, this may backfire badly when exposed to real-time conditions/steps/scenarios.
- ★ During pilot testing, the system is exposed to a limited number of users in the real field. They use the application and give feedbacks on the system.
- ★ These comments come in handy making the application robust enough for the production deployment.

#7) Regulatory Testing

- ✯ This being a healthcare system needs to pass through multiple regulatory/compliance checkpoints.
- ✯ Think of a scenario where the product passes through all the testing steps but fails in the final compliance checklist [testing performed by regulatory body].
- ✯ It is a better practice to get the regulatory requirements in the starting of the development cycle itself. The same should be made part of the testing checklist.
- ✯ By doing that, we make sure the product is certified for the regulatory checklist as well.

#8) Upgrade Testing

- ✯ IoT is a combination of multiple protocols, devices, operating systems, firmware, hardware, networking layers *etc.*
- ✯ When an upgrade is performed, be it for the system or for any of the involved items as stated above, thorough regression testing should be carried out/strategy should be adopted so as overcome upgrade related issues.

IoT Testing Challenges

The challenges a tester faces in IoT are as follows:

#1) Hardware-Software Mesh

IoT is an architecture, which is closely coupled among various hardware and software components. It is not only the software applications that makes the system but also the hardware ones, sensors, communication gateways *etc.* too play a vital role.

Only functionality testing does not help in completely certifying the system. There is always a dependency on each other in terms of the environment, data transfer *etc.* So, it becomes a tedious job as compared to testing a generic system [only software/hardware component].

#2) Device Interaction Module

As this is an architecture between different set(s) of hardware and software, it becomes mandatory that they talk to each other in real time/near real time. When they both integrate with each other, things such as security, backward compatibility, upgrade issues becomes a challenge for the testing team.

#3) Real-Time Data Testing

As we have discussed earlier that a Pilot testing/regulatory testing is mandatory for a system such as this, it also becomes very tough to get such data.

Being in testing team, getting regulatory checkpoints or getting the system deployed in the pilot is very tough. The step becomes even tougher if the system is related to Healthcare as per our example. So, that stays as a big challenge for the testing team.

#4) UI

The IoT is spread across devices belonging to every platform [iOS, Android, Windows, linux]. Now, testing that out on devices can be done but testing it on all possible devices is almost impossible.

We cannot omit the possibility of the UI being accessed from a device which we don't possess or simulate. That's a challenge which is tough to overcome.

#5) Network Availability

Network connection plays a vital role as IoT is all about the data being communicated in faster speeds all the time. IoT architecture has to be tested in all kinds of network connectivity/speeds.

To test this, virtual network simulators are mostly used to vary the network load, connectivity, stability *etc.* But, real time data/network is always a new scenario and testing team doesn't know where the bottleneck would develop in the long run.

IoT Testing Tools

There are various tools which are used during testing IoT systems.

They can be classified based on the target and are given as below:

#1) Software

1. **Wireshark:** This is an Open source application used to monitor the traffic in the interface, source/destination host addresses *etc.*
2. **Tcpdump:** This does a similar job that of the Wireshark except, this does not have a GUI. This is a command line based utility which helps the user in displaying the TCP/IP and other packets that are transmitted or received over a network.

#2) Hardware

1. **JTAG Dongle:** This is similar to a debugger in PC applications. This helps in debugging the target platform code and show variable step by step.
2. **Digital Storage Oscilloscope:** This is used to check various events with time stamps, glitches in power supply, signal integrity check.
3. **Software Defined Radio:** This is used to emulate receiver and transmitter for a large range of wireless gateways.

To the developing world around us, IoT is a growing market and has a lot of opportunities. The time is not far when IoT becomes essential for the testers to survive in the development world.

The IoT-enabled gadget, smart device application, and communication module play a vital role in studying and evaluating the performance and behavior of various IoT services.

Poor design of IoT-enabled devices and services can hamper the correct functioning of the application and in turn negatively affect the end-user experience.

8

Roles of an IoT Professional

IoT Product Manager

This is the professional who focuses on the execution part of the project. His role spans engagement from development to marketing to various routes to market. He/she partners with the development teams to take care of requirements and implementations.

IoT Architect

An architect primary role is to convert ideas into design and design into working code. He/she might not be the actual developer, but is the one that takes up a requirement and then transform them into a solution blueprint or landscape. They map business needs to system & technical requirements.

IoT Developer

This is the hands-on professional who gets down to the basic and creates the actual code.

Industrial Data Scientists

Internet of things generates huge about of data and wherever you find data, you will see a need to have analytics on top of it. This is creating a completely new genre of Data scientists who are experts on working with sensor data. These are professionals that are well versed with data science and are specifically well versed in applying analytics to sensor data and eventually to Internet of things.

Robot Coordinator

The responsibility of robot coordinator will be to supervise the robots on the shop floor and counter any breakdowns or miscalculation. This professional executes both repetitive and disaster recovery duties.

Industrial Engineer

While the IoT developer looks into the software part of IoT stack, industrial engineer takes care of the hardware part of Internet of Things. Hardware is the most important component of Internet of Things stack. Industrial engineer programs Robots and smart devices.

Industrial UI/UX Designer

The top of the IoT stack is dashboards or visual screens that end users look at. These are interfaces that are either used to control the sensors or to examine the data coming out of it.

UI/UX designer would be integral part of the IoT professional ecosystem where this professional would take requirements on the end dashboard and would actually go on to design them.

Chief Internet of Things Officer (CIoTO)

We are yet to see this job title open up, but its imperative that companies in some key industries would find it inevitable to have a c-level job dedicated solely on IoT.

Fuller Stack Developer

IoT pushes developers to go beyond just full stack. Given the complex nature of various components fitting within the whole IoT stack, the developer of future would need to go beyond just software, but also incorporate hardware programming to their skillsets.

Industrial Networking Engineer

This job role requires creative and talented engineers with experience in developing high-quality networking products on schedule. Again, networking is an important component of IoT and we would require separate networking engineers that over time have gathered expertise in developing networking capabilities for IoT devices.

Index

N

O

P

R

S

T

U

www.ingramcontent.com/pod-product-compliance
Ingram Content Group UK Ltd.
Pitfield, Milton Keynes, MK11 3LW, UK
UKHW020047200726
13845UKWH00044B/33

9 789390 384259